When Phones W

and

Lived

RED BOXES

by

Gladys Hobson

A pick and mix assortment
of childhood memories
1939-1953

Illustrations by Gladys Hobson
and cartoonist Gary Lyons

When told that a son of a friend was going to climb Kilimanjaro as part of a project to raise money for a children's education programme to combat AIDS in Africa, I wanted to help. In appreciation of my own childhood, I decided to write this little account of life as I lived it in the 1940's to early 1950's. All income from the book's sale has been promised to the above cause.

All incidents in this book are as I remember them but names may have been changed occasionally to preserve privacy.

Published by Magpies Nest Publishing.
Printed and bound by Stramongate Press, Kendal.

Further copies may be ordered from:
Magpies Nest, Old Hall Drive, Ulverston. LA12 7DG
email: redboxes@thehobsons.co.uk

Or www.ifyouwrite.com.

When Phones Were Immobile
and
lived in
RED BOXES

Contents

Introduction   5

Chapter One   School-days: 7
                 sewage, sex, sport and school dinners

Chapter Two   No NHS   23

Chapter Three   Of God and Bananas   37

Chapter Four   Of war and play   47

Chapter Five   Innocent youth or just plain daft?   61

Chapter Six   Family affairs   75

Chapter Seven   I want to be a designer   85

Chapter Eight   Moving on to where I started!   99

Chapter Nine   Boys!   109

Chapter Ten   You shall go to the ball   119

Conclusion   The beginning of the new   127

Acknowledgements

It isn't easy teaching an old dog new tricks and my thanks go to my son Simon for his patience in the production process of this little book. My thanks also to Norman Price of Manuscript Appraisals for donating his proof-reading skills and to Roy Scott of www.ifyouwrite.com Writers' Showcase for his encouragement and making this book available on his site and donating the income. Gary Lyons turned up at just the right time to add his cartoon humour and I thank him most sincerely.

Introduction

I was waiting in the bank a few days ago when someone's mobile started ringing. A young woman took the phone from her pocket and said to me, "What would we do without them?"

I had to smile. I remember the days before mobiles; when outer space was the realm of Flash Gordon fantasy, and only doctors, businesses and posh people had a telephone installed – the rest of us had to queue at the red box down the road. I was well into my teens before I actually used one. But then, whom could I possibly ring?

It isn't difficult to remember when I first handled a phone. At the time, I was working on the cutting bench in the outerwear department of an old factory in Nottingham. No one in that building could have been more sensitive or naive than I was – nor as incredibly stupid!

One morning the overlooker called me over to his desk.

"A call for you, Gladys," he said.

It was with great fear and trepidation that I took the receiver from him.

"I've never used a phone," I said, my hands shaking. "What do I do?"

"Put that end to your ear and speak in there," he instructed with considerable clarity.

What could be easier?

But my imagination was already working at full speed. My father had been ill for some time; he must be dead! Worse, he'd lost his temper and had done something dastardly! No, it must be my poor mother rushed off to hospital! The house has caught fire, the Trent has flooded, the dog has been run over!

"Yes?" I said into the mouthpiece, fearful of what was to come.

"Gladys?" the voice queried.

"Yes," I said, my mouth dry with anxiety.

"Bring the sheets," the voice demanded.

"What?"

"The sheets, bring the sheets!"

Who was this person demanding sheets? Why should I have sheets, except on my bed? I must have got it wrong.

"The sheets?" I queried, my brain in a whirl and my wet palm gripping the receiver to stop it shaking.

"The sheets!" the voice bellowed. "Bring the bloody sheets. Now!"

Tears were about to run down my face. I turned to the overlooker and handed him the receiver.

"I can't hear what he's saying," I lied.

He took the instrument of torture from my shaking hand. He spoke a few words into the mouthpiece, grinned, and turned to me.

"The wrong Gladys," he said, with an apologetic shrug of his shoulders.

He called to the machinists' overlooker, "Gladys, take the production sheets into the office, please. Mr Raymond wants them."

I had been speaking on the phone to the deputy manager. I hurried to the toilet!

For ages afterwards, I dreaded the phone ringing. But of course, need and ambition force us to adapt and accommodate to modern gadgets.

This little book is a trip down memory lane. Just dip into its pages. If you think it quite unbelievable what we thought and did in those days, believe me, we would have laughed at the very idea of men on the moon and a handy phone in your pocket! As for sex, that was as hush-hush as State secrets. But, delve into these pages and all will be revealed.

Chapter One

School-days: sewage, sex, sport and school dinners

When I was young, it was normal to have single-sex schools. That suited me very well. Boys were loud, rude and dirty. Apart from which, their mothers favoured them, and that made them pushy and arrogant. I dare say we were jealous of our brothers, but why should they get extra helpings of pudding? What did they do that we didn't? We girls were the labourers in the home. We were the good children.

But some senior girls let our school down – the rotters! They were thirteen and should have known better. However, I'm pleased to say the miscreants came from posh homes. They never had anything to do with us lesser mortals, and so we were not dragged into their criminal activity.

We had been given the privilege of touring the new local sewage and waste disposal works. The sewage was very pongy but it was interesting to see what was floating on top – certain rubber objects that were often found in alleys and in the park. Boys would blow them up like balloons. Why would people put balloons down the lavatory? The liquid in the final tank was supposed to be fresh water, and the man said they used it for their tea. As far as I was concerned, it already looked like tea.

We viewed the latest means of recovering scrap metal, had a peek in the fiery furnace and watched them bundling waste paper for recycling. The naughty girls found a package of private letters written by a soldier to his wife and were in fits of giggles as they passed them around for their buddies to read. '*When I come home, you know what*' became words of awe, wonder, thrills and tremendous excitement. The girls were going around telling others that the wife now had a baby – apparently from doing 'You know what'.

But what had the married couple actually done? The girls obviously knew something I didn't and I found that irksome. We outcasts heard that the girls were in big trouble – the wife in question came to school and demanded action or the police would be called in. It was a case of "He-he!" as far as I cared.

As we were expected to leave school at fourteen, we were to begin lessons about sex. What excitement! We were to be introduced to the mysteries of our very existence and that gave us a tremendous feeling of awe.

We gathered in the biology classroom with its long benches and stools, its wall pictures and never-used equipment; its cabinets and raised platform for the teacher's demonstration bench. Compared with the rest of the tatty school, it was a grandiose place of learning. There could be no more fitting stage for the demise of our ignorance and the birth of new knowledge.

Textbooks were given out. We were given the page number. A little embarrassed, but decidedly curious, in silence we turned the pages. What did we find? The life cycle of the single-celled animal!

What a let-down. The biology teacher did not get away with it though. A few pages away we found something very interesting – pictures of frogs mating. So that was how "it" was done!

But if our school was shy about sex, our dog wasn't. Every time she was on heat, she did a lot of humping with her bedding and anything else that happened to be handy. Mother would worry about her. Poor dog; was she being denied release of natural instincts? Should Jenny be allowed to have puppies? Of course, we girls thought puppies would be a very good idea. A large brown and white spaniel-type dog was sniffing around the house at the time. Mother decided he would make a decent mate for Jenny. We opened the side entrance gate to let him in. He didn't oblige. Mother went out and dragged him in! He was introduced to Jenny in the garden and we went inside to let them get on with it. After a while, Jenny started howling. Why howl when she got what she wanted? Mother was now worried that Jenny was being hurt and went out to rescue her. But the deed was over and the borrowed dog was trotting off home. A few days later, my mother saw the borrowed dog with its owner. She told the lady that her dog had got at our dog.

"Really? I would be very interested if she has puppies. He's a very old dog."

Jenny had a beautiful litter. They were all like their dad. Now, was that how babies came to be born? But that did not explain all the touching and kissing business that humans engaged in. Or did it?

Today, I see kids going to school labouring with huge bags on their backs. At my girls' school, I had nothing to take except ingredients on cookery days. Our education was simple: English, arithmetic, geography, history, biology, art, domestic science, sewing, religion and physical education. All textbooks were kept at school and all work was done at school. We had longer hours but life in those days was uncomplicated, in spite of rationing, certain restrictions, and the occasional bomb and air-raid siren.

For a year we had a whole day for learning domestic skills. There was no book learning. It was entirely practical. Half the day, we washed dirty clothes, and ironed with flat irons heated on the range; only the teacher used the one electric iron, which was plugged into the ceiling light. Washing was by hand or by boiling. We rinsed, wrung, rinsed with dolly-blue, wrung, rinsed with starched water, then finally wrung and put to dry on a pulley airer. Dirty clothes were soaked, cuffs and collars scrubbed, and if you accidentally took to school a grubby handkerchief in your washing bag, it had to be given disgusting treatment. Salt-water helps loosen green mucus and it's just not nice before lunch!

We cooked simple dishes. Being wartime, there could be nothing fancy. And with nothing wasted, it was a wonderful foundation for good housekeeping: economical cakes and pastries, nutritious stews and pies. To make our Christmas cake we had to substitute soya for almonds, dates for sultanas, and a mix of condensed milk for icing. It was that good, my brother ate half the cake as soon as I got it home – greedy boy! Sometimes there would be little else than vegetables in the meat and potato pie, but they always looked great with their scalloped edging. And what did it matter if I accidentally used ginger instead of pepper? They were days of making do, pulling together, no complaints and getting on with it.

We had blackberries from the hedgerows, windfall apples from neighbours' trees, cabbages from the allotment, and eggs from our own few hens. My brothers got the double-yoked ones, of course. Occasionally, we had a small share of a pig kept in someone's backyard. Sweets were rationed but we were all the better for it. Mother made our own jam with the sugar ration and she pickled eggs, preserved fruit, preserved the grease from the Christmas goose for our poorly chests in winter, riddled the coal dust to help our fuel ration, and did many other things to keep the home fires burning.

Unfortunately our fires seldom fitted the picture that propaganda merchants liked to get around. Coal rationing made life difficult. There was no central heating. We had no electric fires, and power supplies were uncertain anyway. The kitchen range needed coal for heating water as well as for warmth. Gas pressure was low and would often fall even lower when a cake was in the oven. Our coats hung on the back of the kitchen door – not just as a place to keep them, but to get them dry. Mother would often go down to the coal wharf near the station to beg the coalman to bring us some fuel. It was very rare to have a fire in a room other than the kitchen.

One winter we joined with a number of other desperate people, digging through the wharf's waste heaps to sift out fragments of coal. When a policeman arrived, a stream of women and kids with baskets, mothers with prams and pushchairs with babies sitting on top of nutty-slack, would rush from the site. The policeman would wave his arms and issue threats but no arrests were ever made. It was from cold damp homes that we left for school. School was warm and dry and a good place to be.

Clothes were on coupons. No worry about designer labels in those days; all our clothes bore the utility label. We had been taught at school to make do and mend. So I darned, stitched and patched, unpicked and made new. Everything was a challenge. No worry over what and how much to buy. Bread was brown or white, bacon was lean or fatty, butter was butter and marge was marge. You were allowed your ration and when you shopped, you handed over your ration book and asked for butter, lard, marge, cheese, and sugar. You bought your meat ration and queued for offal and fish. We were taught how to make the most out of what we had, and encouraged to swallow our daily spoonful of free cod liver oil and malt. We never went without and were seldom hungry. When bread was in short supply, our domestic science teacher told us that potatoes were better for us. When the potato crop failed, bread was the healthier food. Our parents and teachers taught us to adapt to circumstances and be satisfied with what we got.

During the long years of food rationing, Mother usually only allowed us to have either marge or jam, but not both, on our bread. Blackcurrant puree became a delicious substitute for jam, and we had it on bread and sometimes on puddings. Some poorer people sold their clothes and sweet coupons; there were always people ready to buy them. In times of emergency, such as a flood, food parcels arrived from the USA. Occasionally, Yanks would hand out goodies and nylons for either favours or out of friendship. Everyone became familiar with SPAM and

different ways of using it. We ate other tinned food, but it could only be purchased using your coupon allowance. Tinned salmon and tinned fruit were especially prized and saved for special occasions. We queued for hours for sausage rolls, pastries and bread, which for most of the time were free of coupons. When soya flour became a good substitute for just about everything, my mother made us sweets and we ate ourselves sick.

The introduction of school milk was great. Before little bottles arrived, it was served to us in beakers. We had it in the large art room. You went through the door, picked up your beaker, drank your milk while you were walking round the room and then went straight out, having put down your empty container. Milk in little bottles was wonderful. When not heated up by the hot radiators, we had ice to crunch.

Then came school dinners. Fantastic! For one shilling (5p) we had a plateful of dinner and a pudding with custard. You were not allowed to leave anything on your plate but that was all right most of the time. However, being a greedy girl, I went back for seconds of a peas and beans mix. They still had some left over. After another helping, I threw up in the lavatory! All that food was so very new to me, and how awful to see it going to waste down the pan!

School discipline was strict but you knew where you were and what you could get away with – nothing! Take a day off and the school-board man would be calling on your parents. Be cheeky and it would be a visit to the horrid headmistress. Pass a book forward or talk at the wrong time and the result was a whack on the hand from Miss Crosby. Stammer on your reading and receive a caustic comment from Miss Smith: "No wonder you failed your eleven-plus oral exam, Gladys. You can do better than that."

A few teachers were warm and friendly and had more creative methods of teaching. School plays and concerts were organised, whereupon my friend and I were daft enough to put on our little acts. When asked to create a natural aquarium in the biology room, we were an hour late getting to another teacher's boring lesson. Our biology teacher was a gem and we would do anything for her. But it isn't what she taught that I remember her for, it is the witness she gave about her baptism. She told us how she went down into the water and came up a changed person. Angels came into it somewhere and the look on her face was quite something. She glowed.

Having failed the eleven plus oral (not surprising when I told them I wanted to be a dancer or an artist) I later passed the test for pupils in their fourteenth year to go to the Nottingham Secondary Art School. It was a two-year course; half the day spent on regular subjects and half doing nothing but art and craft. There were only thirty pupils to a class instead of forty-three or more. I blossomed!

I had a grant for a black blazer and badge, two shirts, a grey jumper and a tie. I bought a second-hand grey skirt for five shillings but it fell to my ankles when the zip broke. To save money, my disabled dad thonged together a grey leather satchel. It was a lovely bit of craftsmanship but everyone else had the usual tan leather ones. Because the uppers of my shoes were worn, my dad stitched on little patches. I felt the shame of poverty terribly, especially when, instead of the uniform navy gabardine, I had only a second-hand pea-green coat to wear. In the playground I stood out like a huge parrot. Needless to say, I wore my blazer throughout most of the two winters.

I had other essential items throughout my schooling: a vest to keep me warm and to give tenuous support to my growing breasts; and that inevitable bastion of defence – our navy-blue bloomers. Unfortunately, they tended to bulge the skirts of the yellow dresses we were allowed to wear in summer. Of course, elastic had a habit of perishing, or breaking free of the stitching, and could let you down badly. Sometimes you had to rely on the leg elastic to spare your blushes. Thankfully, skirts were at mid-calf length! Gym knickers were useful for PE and it was handy to have their secret pocket. With classes of boys at the art school, perhaps they were essential. The girls' lavatory was on a half-landing and the boys had a habit of hanging around the bottom of the staircase. I guess, seeing a bare knee between sock and knickers must have been a very erotic experience, or they would not have risked being caught where they were not allowed. Girls today have got it wrong – too much on display is not necessarily alluring, but what is hidden can send boys wild! I should mention that the headmaster was a bit of a tyrant. He dragged two boys out of their classroom for whistling at my friend and me when we had taken in their crate of milk at playtime, and gave them a good caning for their disgraceful behaviour.

But boys will be boys. Some of them joined the photography club and made the most of the darkroom, or so a friend, who was a member, told me. Since I saw my friend in the arboretum, sitting in a shelter with a boy's hand inside her blazer, I did not find it hard to believe. What did they do in the dark? Frankly, at that time, I thought touching was abhorrent – only allowed by tarts – and I could not understand why she allowed it.

The only time the boys officially mixed with the girls was during the last term of the two-year course. Since it was a two-classroom school with no hall – the other year's two classes would be at the Art College – they joined us for dancing lessons in the YMCA gymnasium. What a lark!

Some of the boys may have acted macho to impress the girls in the playground but when it came to exposing their inadequacies in front of a whole class of girls they were all scared rabbits.

They bunched up together one side of the hall while we girls were at the other. Of course, it has to be said that we had had a bit of practice. But it was not a good thing for us girls to dance together. Both my friend and I were well endowed in the upper regions; we couldn't stop giggling as we constantly bumped our assets.

Being awkward with the dance movements was embarrassing for the boys, but being pressed up to us girls is what the they dreaded most. The teacher was without mercy. When the boys refused to choose a partner, she would grab a lad by the wrist, drag him across the floor, and slap him against a girl, chest to breast! Fearful of the same treatment, the rest of the boys would immediately speed across the room to find a partner.

"You can't dance at a distance. Hold your partner close up," she would bellow, frustrated by the boys' obstinacy.

Of course, they did no such thing. Whatever they might have got up to in the arboretum, in that dance lesson they fought shy of close contact. So the teacher went around slapping the couples together. The boys' hormones inevitably played tricks with their anatomy. Needless to say, we had some very hot and flushed young men in that dancing class.

I can't say we were thrilled at dancing with coy stiff-limbed boys. They seemed to have a habit of practising football tackles in the middle of a quickstep.

But, I have to admit that dancing with the boys was preferable to playing hockey with the girls. One girl in particular had a reputation for knocking out the front teeth of her opponents with her hockey stick. Apparently she never fouled; it was the others who got in the way! She would carve a path through the opposition like a hot knife through butter. Scaredy-cat girls like me just ran out of her way and hoped she would trip up on her own hockey stick. I can see that girl now: reddish long fuzzy hair, a wild look on her face, a strong athletic build and a bombastic talker who seldom had a nice thing to say about anyone – well, at least, not about me! But I must admit I was useless at hockey. When I did get the ball passed to me I always managed to hit it straight to the opposition.

I was hopeless at swimming too. When practising a roll at the side of the bath to get us used to our head being under water, I would inevitably end up like a duck – head down, bottom up – and have to be pulled out. The teacher got used to receiving my not-well-this-week notes, and either thought I had a major period problem or accepted I was a serious risk to her teaching career.

At my previous school I was part of the netball team - that is, when the regulars failed to turn up. I must have been the only shooter that never scored a goal in a match. At least, I was keen. I practised shooting at my friend's house. We found an old bent iron ring discarded from a netball post. My dad put it back into shape and my friend and I, between us, fixed it to a drainpipe in the courtyard of their big house. I don't think leather balls were available in wartime – we could not have afforded one if they were. Plastic ones did not exist. So I made a ball out of oilcloth table covering. It was a trial and error method of making a pattern. Eventually, about eight segments roughly made up the spherical shape. I stitched it together on our ancient Singer, stuffed it with kapok, hand-stitched the gap, and we had the perfect ball to practice our shooting technique. Perfect, that is, to ensure remarkable accuracy in the courtyard with no opposition, and just the job to make sure I would never score in matches! The weight, shape and feel of the ball were all just too different. Of course there is a simpler reason for not scoring. I was useless!

I was no better at athletics. Fancying myself as a high jumper, I nearly injured my back. Entering for the hurdles, I did not even reach the finishing line. I managed to knock down every hurdle, bruise my legs and fall flat on my face. Try running and I always came last. But, one thing I was terrific at was the three-legged race. Unfortunately it was not a school event, but in local community competitions my friend and I won every time. It was not because we were good runners, but because we spent hours practising on their large lawn. It was a lesson in coordinating our movements, especially as we were a little and large couple.

I may not have been the athletic type, but I did well in all academic and creative

subjects. Of course, lessons were totally different to today's approach to learning. No computers, no televisions, and although most people had a wireless, it was not something we had in schools. It was mostly chalk and talk with the occasional visit. On one occasion we were taken to see *Henry V* at a city cinema but I was so bored I dropped off to sleep!

Our art classes were fantastic: lettering, nature drawing, memory and imagination, weaving, fabric printing, dress design, dress decoration, pattern cutting, dressmaking and others. We were a privileged few and proud to have been chosen. I guess being happy at school and rightly placed – perhaps a lesson for today's education system – ensured we all worked hard. I shone in every subject.

Towards the end of the final year, the whole school of one hundred and twenty pupils went on a visit to London. We caught an early morning train and set off on what for me was a great adventure. I had never been so far away from home. But, although we had a very interesting time in the great city, what was most memorable was what happened on the way home.

Unfortunately, our group, along with two others, missed the train. This was more of a devastating blow for our nice teacher than it was for us. She was the one the head was most furious with. I can see him now, pacing the platform with wrath distorting his face into an ugly grimace. If he had had his cane with him I'm sure he would have whacked the lot of us. Buses that were meeting the train had to be rescheduled to allow for our late arrival. A lot of telephoning had to be done to change the arrangements. The majority of parents could not be contacted because few people had telephones in those days and there was considerable concern about pupils getting home very late.

By the time the train steamed into Nottingham station and we boarded our buses to take us home it was very late indeed. I was very tired but some of the pupils were being very lively; a lot of kissing was going on and a bit more besides. This in spite of having a responsible adult in charge of us. A student teacher nicknamed Mr Inkwell, who had helped supervise the groups of schoolchildren, was on the bus to make sure we got to our individual bus stops safely. We girls, now fifteen, thought he was fantastic. I sat there tired and dreamy, thinking about this gorgeous guy who was sitting up on the top deck.

I was also wondering why girls were coming down the stairs and going back up with one or two others. At first I thought it was just the lads getting a bit of what they wanted, but it soon became obvious what the main attraction for that evening was. Each time students left the bus, it was Inkwell's job to make sure they did so safely. He came down the stairs and before reaching the bus stop, girls were giving him a final kiss before parting. They were nearly all at it. I was feeling quite jealous but I was much too shy to do anything about it. I never knew if the headmaster found out but we didn't see Inkwell again!

I was never a popular girl at our art school. I was far too shy to make many friends and no other girls came from my area of Beeston. I had a lovely friend called Olive, but she left early when her family moved. I also had a friend called Mary. She was the one I danced with at school – you might say that we were bosom friends! Mary had a very close boyfriend called Pinter whose hormones were well developed, and who had a friend called Jake. It was inevitable that the four of us would occasionally meet up in the arboretum during our lunch breaks.

One lunchtime, the know-it-all Pinter was giving us the benefit of his knowledge concerning fighting and self-defence. He asked me to stand up so he could demonstrate a point. Gullible as usual, I obliged. He took my arm and twisted it round my back, causing me to howl in pain, and then cry like a baby as he held on to it. In absolute fury, Jake jumped on him and started to beat him up.

Swinging his fists, my hero yelled, "Leave her alone, you swine!"

It was the first time I had seen Jake in action – any action. I was very impressed and my opinion of him went up a few notches. It was a rotten thing that Pinter had done and I couldn't understand why Mary went out with him. The fact that she was grinning throughout the whole episode probably meant that she enjoyed the excitement he engendered.

As you might expect from a sensual person like Pinter, he was always ready to tell dirty stories and raunchy jokes. I laughed along with the others, mainly because I didn't want to show my ignorance. For in truth, being ignorant about sexual matters, I was not aware of the significance of most dirty jokes.

Every time Pinter saw a male with his hands in his pockets, he would laugh and say that he was playing pocket billiards. I twigged the possibility of a willie being used like a billiard cue, although the only male genital organs I had seen were those of babies, a young boy's pencil-like object, and a man's rubbery hose-pipe thingy (he was peeing up our house wall at the time). But billiards needed balls as well. Was Pinter saying that certain males went around with balls in their pockets to get their willies excited? Better to laugh than ask questions and become the fall guy for his jokes. I would be the laughing stock of the whole school.

Children can be so cruel. A few months earlier, I'd had a chair pulled away from under me when I was about to sit down. It had happened one wet lunchtime when the room was full of boys as well as girls. I fell badly and it was an incredibly painful and humiliating experience. The prefect told the boy off but the room was already full of shouts of glee and laughter.

In many ways I was a romantic young lady. With the cinema providing the main entertainment in the nineteen-forties, I saw a lot of films and I had my heartthrobs just like other girls did. In those days, actors in films were only allowed to kiss; touching and any other sexual activity was absolutely forbidden.

But eye contact and kissing was enough to stir the young female heart. I would fantasise about such things. Since I had nothing to put in my diary, I once wrote that I was not sure of my love for Jake. Of course, someone at school grabbed my diary and read out the only words in the book. It was lunchtime and Jake was in the classroom. I was mortified. Nearly everyone was laughing but he was looking very pleased with himself. Poor lad, what sort of message did it give him? No way did I love him.

Before the end of our two years, Jake raised the courage to give me a kiss. Pinter, who was doing very nicely with Mary, had been trying to get him to do it for ages. In a way, I wanted him to kiss me because he was a nice boy – even if he was stiff and awkward. But I have to confess that his pimples put me off. His face was a little bristly too, because shaving would have made his pus-filled spots worse.

We were in the arboretum when he finally summoned up enough courage. Pinter was having a sloppy session with Mary to show him the way. Not that Jake required showing but he certainly needed encouraging.

"Come on, Jake, it's now or never. She's standing waiting. Do you want me to show you how?"

Pinter grabbed hold of me, but Jake yelled, "No! You leave her alone."

"Do you mind if I kiss you, Gladys?" he asked nervously.

I felt like saying, "Get on with it!" Instead I whispered, "No, I don't mind."

I closed my eyes and waited. He didn't put his arms around

me. He just came close up and bent his head to reach me. I felt the touch of his lips on mine, along with a slight brushing of the short bristles of his chin and upper lip. I knew the horrid pus-filled spots were close to my flesh but I tried not to be repulsed by them. And that was it. After we left school, we never met again.

Chapter Two

No NHS

If ever I feel like grousing about our National Health Service, I dig out of my memory bank of how things used to be. Fortunately for our family, my dad paid into something or other that took care of some medical bills.

During the Second World War we had a lovely old doctor, Dr Bonner. He had served as an army doctor during the earlier war, and was well beyond retirement age. He loved children and gave us little pieces of fruit cake sent to him from South Africa, and let us pick the bluebells from his vast garden. He also showed us inside his underground air-raid shelter, built in a clearing a little way from his huge house. He always gave us time and made a fuss of us. If he had been practising today, the way he examined me when I had chickenpox – as if it had invaded my intimate parts – might well have brought his motives under scrutiny.

But he wasn't the only dodgy friendly doctor. Some years later I had to visit a consultant chest specialist. Alone in his room, he had me sitting in a chair opposite him. We were in front of a roaring coal fire. He slipped my vest straps off my shoulders while he examined my chest in fine detail. Then, still sitting in the chairs, he pulled me up to him while he examined my back with his stethoscope. I was practically on his knees, pressed hard to his chest with my head on his shoulder, his Brylcreem strong in my nostrils.

One day, when I was getting better after a serious illness, Dr Bonner came to see me. Afterwards he took me with him in his car while he visited a few sick people. A girl sent me out one of her precious oranges. It was the first time I had been in a car and I had not had such exotic fruit for ages. Only infants and the sick were allowed to have oranges. Like all food coming from abroad during the sinking of supply ships, they were in very short supply.

With Dr Bonner's casual approach to time, it was hardly surprising if patients could wait for two hours or more to see him. The situation was made worse because he dispensed his own medicines: counting out pills and pouring out colourful liquid – usually pink linctus, iron tonic or brown cough medicine – out of huge jars into small bottles. Of course, there were no antibiotics, and for painkillers we just had aspirins. Mother made bread poultices to draw out boils, rendered goose-grease for chesty coughs, and we all had good old TCP to gargle with and tackle any other problem. We only went to old Bony, or he came to us, if all else failed or we were very poorly indeed.

But if there was a long wait, there were compensations. Our doctor had dramatic pictures on his waiting-room walls. These were no tatty posters concerned with health warnings, or advertisements of groups and associations there to support and advise. I can only remember such things existing in public lavatories where we were all expecting to get VD if we sat on the seats. No, these were framed prints hung on each wall – a veritable picture gallery.

The one I liked the best was of a man being punished by being publicly sawn in half. On reflection, it may be that he was going through the last stages of the traitor's fate – the dreaded drawing and quartering. On the other hand, it might have been a surgeon's very public demonstration of his skill with knife and saw. That, and the other pictures, set our young imaginations alight, giving us sober food for thought whilst waiting for our kindly Dr Bonner to give us his personal attention. Yes, it was worth the wait just to view the doctor's art gallery.

Hospitals were places you never wanted to enter; people died in them! Surgery was not advised unless it was considered a dire necessity. When I was just turned twelve, I went with my mother to see my dad after he'd had his hernia fixed. He was in the large surgery ward of Nottingham City Hospital. It was packed with very poorly people secured in neatly-made beds. The nurses, in starched white uniforms, made sure there were only two visitors to each bed and that they all left at the ring of the bell. Young children were not allowed inside. Just as well perhaps, because by the door was a young man with meningitis. He was a terrible sight, his eyes wild and his whole body shaking. There was a strong smell of disinfectant about the place but it failed to hide all the other smells. My dad's wound had turned septic and the pus was making a bit of a stink. The man in the bed next to my dad was dying. The whole atmosphere was depressing and there was no privacy. I expect the nurse had to be able to see around the whole ward. The only happy thing out of the visit was to see my dad and know that he was getting his nightly bottle of stout.

But I was not totally shocked by the hospital scene. I had been in hospital myself, twice.

I had just turned seven. It was December 1939 and the war had recently started. And my own happy little world was about to be shattered.

I had been sitting at my desk working away at my lessons, when the teacher came up close to me and looked at my face. She seemed quite alarmed and wanted to know how I was feeling. She sent for the headmistress. Between them, it was decided that I should be taken to the clinic for a medical opinion. No doubt they were mostly concerned to know if I had a contagious disease and wanted to get me away from the rest of the children. The clinic confirmed that I had Scarlet Fever. In those days, it was a notifiable disease and regarded as being quite dangerous. Years ago there were no antibiotics or medicines to cure such diseases. The body had to heal itself with the help of rest and healthy food. Complete isolation of the patient was needed. For the unlucky ones, like myself, this had to be in an isolation hospital.

My adult brother, Jack, caught the disease too, but he refused to go away. Mother had to nurse him at home, keeping him isolated in his bedroom until he was better. She had to take him his meals, water to wash with, and empty his smelly chamber-pot every day so he didn't use the bathroom. It was the only time she ever smoked cigarettes! The whole house had to be fumigated to prevent the disease spreading.

After being taken to the clinic, I was taken home and handed over to my mother and our own doctor was contacted as soon as possible. By the time the doctor arrived I was tucked up in bed wondering what was going to happen to me. After the doctor had done his examination, he took my mother over to the window to have a quiet word with her. They had little looks towards the bed and I could see that my mother was looking very worried. I heard the doctor talking about hospital and eventually saw my mother nodding her head in agreement.

Sure enough, when the doctor left, my mother came back upstairs to tell me that I was going to be taken to hospital.

"Don't worry, Luvvy, I'll come and see you. You'll soon be home again."

But I did worry. It all felt strange and unreal. Soon the ambulance arrived. I heard it stop outside the bedroom window. There was a knock at the door, the sound of voices in the hall, footsteps on the stairs, and then a uniformed man came into the room. He rolled me in a blanket with my arms by my sides, threw me over his shoulder, and took me down to the street and into the ambulance. I began to live in a timeless world away from everything and everyone I knew and loved. I was very poorly and exceedingly unhappy, but I tried not to cry.

I was taken to the isolation hospital miles away into the country. There I was put to bed in the women's ward. As a young child I had little control over my life but in that place, I had none.

I was put in an end bed next to a girl who was about twelve years old. I was too young for her to talk to me. Except for a baby in a cot, we were the only children in a ward of adults. I was next to the nurses' small office. Since there was a window in the wall, I could just see into the room, at least, the upper part of it. There was a clock on the wall. By patients asking me to tell them where the hands were, I was soon able to tell the time. At least, it was a bit of education and the only sort I was going to receive for a while. There were no books to look at or toys to play with.

After the first night in hospital, I wet the bed. I felt such a big baby. No one was cross with me but I felt the shame of it keenly. What would my parents and the rest of the family think?

I was to spend the first two weeks in bed. Then, for another four weeks, I would be allowed to get up and dress each day. I was given a very odd garment to wear in bed. It had sleeves and legs, buttoned right down the front, and had a buttoned flap at the back so that I could use the bedpan without having to get undressed. I hated it, especially that silly flap.

The bedpan was quite new to me and seemed a very strange shape. In those days they were made of enamel and shaped like frying pans with a hollow handle and rim. I hated having to sit on them in full view of other patients. It was terribly embarrassing when I made a smell, then having to wait for the nurse to come and get rid of the pan and its contents.

It must have been the first day after my arrival at the hospital that I called for the nurse, as I thought I had been told to.

"Nurse, nurse, I need the bread pan," I called. Afraid of wetting the bed, I yelled for the pan again. "Nurse, nurse, I need the bread pan."

The nurse came with the pan, plus a broad smile on her face.

"What did you ask for?"

"The bread pan", I answered, nearly in tears because everyone was laughing.

She burst into fits of laughter and so did the ladies in their beds.

"*Bedpan*, Gladys," she said. "You use it in bed."

I had, of course, merely repeated what I thought I had heard, without reasoning as to what it meant in the context of how it was being used. Since it was shaped like a frying pan, it was not unreasonable to think it was a pan for frying bread in. I felt exceedingly stupid. Knowing what went into it, of course they would not use it for cooking!

Every morning we had a banana for breakfast. They must have been some of the precious few available before the war was over. Funny, as I write, I can actually smell the banana and taste the bread that came with it. Early morning, a nurse would wake me up so that I could use the bedpan. She would ask me if I'd had my bowels moved. Bowels moved? What were they and who would move them? No doubt she explained. If I said no, then I was given some horrid black medicine and told to eat my breakfast banana with it. So I only had the piece of bread for breakfast. It seemed a long time until dinner-time. The food was terrible. Usually mince for dinner, and bread and jam for tea, unless the patients had their own eggs for the nurses to boil for them.

My parents were the only permitted visitors. They had to talk to me through the glass windows. Visiting was for thirty minutes, twice a week. Only my mother could get to visit me in the week and sometimes father would come with her on Saturdays. Although it was a two-bus journey and the weather was very bad, my mother always came. Once a week I was given a sixpence to buy pop. Altogether, it must have been a very expensive time for my mother.

I had been in hospital nearly two weeks and I was going to be allowed out of bed to go to the Christmas party. My mother had been asked to bring me some clothes to wear for the occasion. She forgot and I was bitterly disappointed. It must have been very hard for my mother because she would have known how I felt and she could not even give me a cuddle.

The nurse said that I could wear a hospital dressing gown to go to the party in. My parents thought that would make me happy and were able to go home feeling that all was well. But all was not well. I was feeling utterly sad and alone. I wanted to be home with my family, not in that strange place where I was continually being teased that there were crickets in my bed. I wanted to be back in bed with my sister and to have someone to play with. I did not like bedpans, or being woken up to take nasty medicine. I wanted my mother. But I did not say so. I did not say anything.

I put on the dressing gown and began the lonely walk to the party in the men's ward, on the other side of the hallway. I felt utterly, utterly, alone and unsure of myself. Would they laugh at me in a dressing gown? I did not know much about parties as we never had any at home. There had been a school party once. We wore our best clothes and I knew the children and teachers. Now I was in a dressing gown and I had no friends. I was overwhelmed by misery.

Tears trickled down my cheeks as I passed the nurses' office door.

"What's the matter with you?" asked a nurse when she saw and heard me cry.

I did not know what to say. Wanting my mother and to go home, were things that must never be said.

"I'm cold," I lied.

She threw a blanket at me. "What a big baby. Put this round you and stop crying."

Stung by the rebuke, I did as I was told. Thinking that I looked even more stupid with a blanket wrapped around me, I pushed open the door to the men's ward and walked up to the table where everyone was about to start the party. There was just the one empty seat.

Before long we were all pulling crackers. Someone helped me to pull mine. I looked for the little toy. There was none.

"Gladys hasn't got anything in her cracker", said the person next to me.

"Gladys doesn't deserve anything," said the nurse who had thrown me the blanket.

Now everyone would know that I was a bad girl.

I was beginning to experience the harsh realities of life beyond the security of my home and family. I must not cry. I must not show how I feel. I must be good. I did not know the word rejection but I felt it just the same. I did not know the meaning of isolation but I was experiencing it. That hospital was built to keep seriously diseased people apart from the rest of the community in order to avoid epidemics. But it also had an effect of promoting a deep sense of individual isolation, and of being unclean and unwanted.

The Christmas party over, I went back to bed in the women's ward and waited for Santa to come. I had a brown baby doll in my bag. I was asked to let the crying baby play with it. The baby pulled its head off and then messed on its body.

When allowed out of bed, I watched snow falling outside of the window and looked for footprints on the soft white carpet. I waited for my parents to visit. I waited for the sixpence. I waited to go home.

At last, after six long weeks, the day arrived when my mother brought my outdoor clothes. The clothes that I had worn in hospital, along with my small collection of personal things, were stoved. I put my clothes on in the office. I had to wear almost two of everything. It was a cold day and snow still lay on the ground. It was my first time out for six weeks and there was a long journey home. I stepped outside into the sweet fresh air. I was free! I was with my mother. I was holding her hand. I was going home!

Later that year, my brother was rushed into hospital. He had been suffering a lot of pain with appendicitis. The doctor sent for an ambulance. By the time he reached the hospital, his appendix had burst and the whole area had become numb. The surgeon went straight ahead with the operation and only gave him a whiff of something when the feeling returned during the operation. I was very impressed with my brother's bravery.

But it was only another year or so before I had another hospital experience. Before the days of penicillin, tonsillitis was a painful and debilitating problem. The popular cure was to have them removed, along with your adenoids. Lured by the promise of ice-cream and jelly, I agreed to be treated - not that I had a choice!

Along with my sister, Mother took me to hospital where she handed us over to a nurse. We were herded with other children into a ward that consisted of two rows of iron-framed beds. Before long, we were dressed in gowns and waterproof hats. When we were all ready, we were taken to a waiting room that had a seat running around all four walls.

Two nurses kept us singing with loud voices. Every few minutes a door opened and a child was taken out. So we had to sing all the louder. *"Ten green bottles"* might have been more appropriate than the *"White cliffs of Dover"*!

My turn came – not many of us singing by this time! The door opened. Someone took my hand and, trembling with fear, I was walked to the other side of a corridor. A door opened the way to the operating theatre. I saw the high narrow table, overhung with brilliant lights and surrounded by people in white gowns wearing masks and head coverings. I was lifted onto the table and had something placed over my mouth. I was frightened; I couldn't get my breath. I opened my mouth and screamed.

I woke up lying on a bed. An enamel bowl was wedged against my mouth to catch the blood trickling from my nose and throat. I hurt badly. I looked down the line of beds. Each child was like me: head at the bottom of the bed resting on a rubber sheet, and with a bowl bright with blood. Some children were crying for their mummies; some were moaning or whimpering. None was eating ice-cream and jelly! Occasionally the sound of a bowl falling on the floor brought a nurse scurrying to mop up the blood. Someone would come round wiping mouths to see if the bleeding had stopped. To my young mind, it was a scene from hell!

Next morning we were all lying in bed the right way round and a doctor came to examine our throats. If we were healing all right, we could go home.

Not long after getting home, my sister was found to have

chickenpox and a little later, I too had the same infection. I do not know which was worse, the sore throat or the dreadful itching!

Immunisation had arrived and we were given injections to save us from diphtheria and smallpox. The site of the injection swelled and spread out into a large painful circle and I felt a little unwell. But having suffered from all the other childhood diseases – and they were very debilitating – it was worth the price.

But disease was not the only public health concern. Wartime conditions spread parasites that lived under the skin. Not long after being in hospital, along with my mother and sister I had to pay a visit to a cleansing centre. I was in the grip of utter shame and humiliation. I had scabies!

I could not tell my classmates why I was not at school. My closest friend's mother, possibly worried her children might catch whatever I had, continually quizzed me.

"Come on, Gladys, what's the matter with you?"

"Summer rash, I think," I would say, hiding my hands with their tell-tale scratch marks.

"Don't be shy; you can tell us. We won't think you're a spy if you've got German measles!"

"I've eaten too many plums and they've given me an itchy rash."

By that time I was not contagious. I had already been cleansed.

The clinic was set up in an old village school. We had to catch two buses to get there. I felt like an unclean outcast. The nurses were kindly enough but the procedure was very humiliating. I had to strip and take a hot bath. Then, while I stood in the bath completely naked, the nurse used a big shaving brush to cover me with a creamy substance. I had to part my legs while she worked the stuff into every crack and cranny. I then had to wave my arms about to get the stuff to dry. Even while the cream was still damp on my body, I was told to dress and run around the old playground. Although in a fairly isolated spot, I was frightened of being seen by someone who knew us.

If I thought that experience humiliating, there was even worse to come. When I moved up to the girls' school, I managed to pick up head lice. The headmistress had a policy of name and shame. The nit nurse visited the school at regular intervals. Fear gripped the whole class when she walked into the classroom. You stood in a line while she parted your hair, hoping that your name would not go down in her little black book. Knowing what was going to happen, some children would sit down crying. In the morning at the end of assembly, the head would read aloud the name of every pupil on the nurse's list.

"These girls have dirty heads. Stay away from them."

During the war years, many children were infected with head lice. We were constantly using a nit comb. It was a bit like going fishing. With a sheet of newspaper on the floor, we would kneel and comb through our hair, watching the lice fall and run. We picked them up and killed them between our thumbnails. How many caught today? Then the eggs, sticking on to hairs, had to be removed. With the usual hair washing, using soap with a vinegar rinse – no fancy shampoos in those days – we had a bottle of stuff from the chemist to help us clean up. But we still managed to keep picking up the little beasties. When my name was read out, I could have wept for shame. Girls close to me moved further away. Once more, I was unclean!

What joy when my name was no longer read out. I heard a girl standing behind me whisper, "Gladys is off the list."

Worms too, became a menace. With the shortage of paper in the school lavatories and less-than-perfect washing facilities, it was easy for an epidemic to break out. London evacuees were always blamed, but that was unfair. With our cold damp house and lack of hot water, I could be just as scruffy as anyone else could. The nit nurse told me off for having a dirty neck.

"Well, soap's on ration," my friend's mother said, when told of my disgrace. I thought she might have been thinking of her own neck.

No way was I going to strip down to wash in freezing cold conditions. Some nights the water pipes, which ran under our bed, froze. So much ice gathered on the window pane, it was hard to scratch it off. My sister would come home from night shift and snuggle up to my sister and me. She was incredibly cold. We had hot-water bottles and heated bricks in the beds, but we still put our clothes on top of the quilt to keep us warm. We didn't want our clothes to be frozen either! As it was, I suffered severe chilblains every winter.

Having outside lavatories probably helped spread worms and diseases. Our baker, who called several times a week, always used our back lavatory. He never once washed his hands, even though bread was unwrapped in those days. Other callers – tea vendor, milkman, greengrocer, sweep, insurance man and various collectors of money – were just the same. Food was handled in shops but no one complained. People had their chamber pots under their beds, as did we, but there was no washing of hands afterwards. During the night, the bathroom was only used in summer. It was a cold dark trip to both light-switch and bathroom. Many people only had an outdoor lavatory. So why bother going out in the rain and frost?

Unless there was an attendant, public lavatories left much to be desired. They could get very smelly. The containers for dirty sanitary towels tended to fill up. Having no bin liners or bags to put discarded objects in, made the situation worse. I once saw the refuse collector come out of the ladies' lavatories carrying an armful of the smelly objects.

My father was disabled and there were no special lavatories

or facilities of any kind. Every time my mother pushed him out in his wheelchair they had to carry an empty milk bottle with them.

There was little help for the disabled when I was young. Being so helpless after a very active working life, made my father very bad tempered. His wheelchair had a mind of its own and would occasionally veer to the right. Whilst being pushed around Nottingham University Park, several times he nearly landed in the lake with the fish.

"Your mother's trying to bloody drown me!" he was wont to yell.

Unable to get to work to do his job, he was forced to retire on sick benefit – very little in those days. Mother had a number of cleaning jobs and Dad tried to earn money by working from home – shoe repairs, leather work, motor restoration, and relining baby prams. Weary with pain and immobility, he became very frustrated when things went wrong. The air became blue with his language and Mother suffered much verbal abuse. Home was not always a happy place to be. Even at night, I sometimes heard my dad yell with agonising cramp.

"Give me a knife so I can cut the bloody thing off!"

Sometimes, when he was poorly, we went out at night to find an open fish and chip shop where we would queue for hours to get his favourite food. Because he was hurting, we hurt too.

With others, my dad struggled to get disabled people motorised vehicles and, eventually, the government provided them. They were only single-seated and some of the most dangerous vehicles on the road but at least he was mobile. Thankfully, we now have a more caring society.

The cleansing clinic

Chapter Three

Of God and bananas

"For thou wilt be done," I recited every morning at school.

How could we say that God would be done? Mrs Mop of BBC's ITMA, said in every programme, "Can I do you now, sir?" and everyone would laugh. Whatever that cleaning lady did to Tommy Handley was a cause for mirth. Was God, too, in for some hilarious treatment? It all seemed highly irreverent to me. Just saying the words made me feel slightly wicked.

Throughout my schooling, every day began with some kind of religious assembly and, most days, with a religious education lesson. In those days, in my schools, God was not discussed or questioned. God was. Why doubt the fact of his eternal existence? We had our oldest textbook, the Bible, assuming his presence. No matter how bad the war reports reaching us via the radio or newspapers – they were just a few sheets in those days – we never doubted the outcome. After all, God was on our side. He knew when we were bad and he knew when we were good. He was an all-seeing, all knowing presence, the headmaster-on-high ready to punish but also the heavenly father who loved us. For years I could live with this dichotomy. After all, my own father was just the same. Dad may never have thrashed us but the threat was there. In those days, it was probably true for most children. I certainly knew of no other kind of child-father relationship within my circle of friends. And I said my prayers at night as a matter of routine. What might happen if I did not do so?

As far as I can remember, I had never been inside a church until the day my sister took me with her to Sunday school. It was a Four Square Elim Church. Though what it meant I had no idea. I know now that it was a Pentecostal Church, but at that young age it was merely a pleasant place to go on a Sunday.

A lot of children went to Sunday school in those days. With nothing else to do in particular, it was somewhere to go. We had picnic outings, occasional treasure hunts, and the annual

Anniversary. We had stories read to us, followed by quizzes. We sang jolly songs and did all the actions that went with them. The Pastor taught us a song in Spanish, which I remember to this day. We thought it great to speak a foreign language. It was all good fun when I was very young. I enjoyed the stories and the singing. But eventually, as I grew older, I became tired of songs for the very young and, not being old enough for the Bible class, I drifted away. By that time I had found more exciting things to do.

As a young child, with no such things as televisions or electronic games to keep us at home (nor did we have a family car to take us on trips) the Sunday school outings really meant something to us. They were also a substitute for the holidays we never had. A furniture van would take us off into the country and we would picnic and have races on a farm. What did it matter if it rained? There was the barn. What did it matter if the field was full of cow-pats? It was fun decorating them with flowers, twigs, and stones, to make them look like the birthday cakes we never had.

In 1941, I was given my very first Bible. I still have it, complete with my first attempts at joined-up writing stating my name and address on the inside cover. The Bible was seldom used, but twenty years later it took on great significance in my life.

The Bible was offered to children who had made a promise to Jesus. It was this promise that has powerfully affected my life, although at the time it may not have appeared that way.

One Sunday afternoon at the Sunday school, instead of us going into our individual classes, all the children sat together in the pews where the adult congregation sat for services. It was a special day because the Pastor wanted to talk directly to all the children. He was a nice friendly man and was good at telling stories. That day, he told us a story that I have never forgotten - at least, not the essential thread of it.

The Pastor told us about a sick little boy called Billy. Billy had always been a happy child who loved his home and especially his parents. He also loved Jesus because the Bible told him that He was his special friend. The lad always knew that Jesus was close to him and sometimes he would talk with Him. The pastor said that talking to Jesus was called prayer. But to little Billy it was just talking and being with someone who loved him. In a very special way, Billy had given his heart to Jesus and he knew that Jesus would be his friend for ever.

Billy's parents knew from the day that Billy was born that their child had not long to live. They were told to love and enjoy him and make the most of the time they had together. Billy was their only child and they believed that he was a gift from God. Although deeply sad that Billy would leave them, they knew that God would look after him and that one day they would all be together again.

Billy did not want to leave his mummy and daddy but he knew that he was dying. He was getting weaker and weaker every day.

Sitting in my pew, I followed the story in minute detail. I could see the sick child in a bed like mine, in a room like mine, in a home like mine.

"Boys and girls, was Billy frightened?"

A few whispered yes but some shouted, "No!"

"Quite right. Billy was not afraid of dying because he knew that Jesus would be near him wherever he went. He trusted his friend to be with him forever. Billy would never be alone."

That meant something to me. It had not been so very long since I had been lonely in hospital with no real friend to talk to. I was listening intently.

The Pastor continued. "One night Jesus came into Billy's bedroom. He lifted Billy into his arms and carried him to another room to live with him forever. A place where he would no longer suffer and where no one could harm him. A place where he would always be happy."

That sounded like a pretty good deal to me.

"Now, I'm going to ask you to close your eyes. Put up your hand if you would like to give your heart to Jesus, and I will say a prayer for each one of you."

I closed my eyes, put up my hand, and heard the prayer. I

repeated what I was told to say and it was all over. I had given my heart to Jesus and He would always be my friend.

Excited, I ran home to tell my mother that I had given my heart to Jesus.

"That's nice", she said, and that was that.

But something else happened that had a powerful influence on the early growth of my spiritual life.

One day Grandfather Brock, my father's father, came to visit us. It was the only time that I was to see any of my grandparents and the memory of doing so is clear in my mind.

I knew that Grandfather was a very special person and that it was something to do with him working in the church. What he did, I could not really fathom because 'church' was a big mystery to me. Actually, he ran the Seamen's Mission in Scarborough. My father said that he was a parson, something like the pastor at the chapel. We were told to behave ourselves and keep out of the way as he'd come to talk to our dad.

I did not see Grandfather arrive but I knew that he was in the sitting room because I could hear voices. It all seemed very mysterious and since there was no one around to see me, I listened at the door.

Grandfather was talking about heaven. He told my father that he had been there and what a wonderful place it was. I heard him say that he had met friends who had died, and that death was nothing to be afraid of. I thought he must be very special. I asked mother if I could see him. She told me to knock at the door.

An elderly gentleman with a white beard stood up and gently shook my hand. He seemed kind and friendly and I was very impressed by his stature; he towered over me. I was rather awed to be in his presence. This was someone who knew all about God and heaven, and he was my grandfather! I did not see him again but he was now a part of my life. Later, I read a book containing a chapter about my grandfather, of how he had been in William Booth's Christian Mission before it became the Salvation Army, and I was even more impressed. My grandfather laboured to save souls and heal their bodies in the name of Jesus. God was beginning to emotionally connect with my life. The hymns we sang at school took on a deeper meaning.

I may not have questioned the existence of God, but one day, early in the war, I decided to try out the efficacy of prayer. At the time I was sitting in the outside lavatory, a whitewashed nook of a place, with only the customary strung squares of newspaper and an old banana box for company. It was a private retreat, fine for dreaming while waiting for stubborn muscles to perform. The pictures of bananas on the top of the box made me long for one. It had been ages since they were available. The last time I saw one was when a girl brought one to school. Her soldier brother had brought it back from abroad. She had eaten the fruit herself and divided the skin between her friends. The rest of us had to make do with just the smell.

I decided to ask God for a banana.

"God, if you can do everything, turn this picture into a real banana."

I slowly opened my eyes and, of course, there was no banana. I suddenly felt a wave of shame spread over me. What a wicked girl! We can't tell God what to do. We don't ask for things we do not need, and we do not put him to the test. I may not have received a banana but I had a deep inner conviction of his holy and powerful presence. I did not have to trust that God existed; I somehow knew he did. Of course, my feelings may have been reflecting my relationship to my father!

I once heard my father telling someone about his near death experience. Evidently, while working at Chilwell Ordnance Depot, he was trapped between two trucks. When he was released, having no signs of life, he was thought to be dead. They spread him out on the ground and waited for the ambulance. My father said that he was floating above them listening to what was being said about him. When medical help arrived, he was brought back to life.

Mother used to say that little pigs have big ears. I had the biggest of the lot. Picking up information in snippets can be a bad thing. When I was young, I imagined a world of ghosts existing with and around us. I became frightened of the dark. With the wartime blackout and lack of lighting in and outside the home, I dreaded dark nights. I would close my eyes going down the passage from the kitchen until I felt the electric light switch at the bottom of the stairs. And repeat the process to get to my bedroom. When I had to put a shilling in the meter because the light had gone out, I would have my eyes shut tight until light made it impossible to see my imaginary ghosts. During winter, I did a lot of feeling my way in the dark with my eyes closed.

In my own mind, my fear was justified because I had seen a ghost. At least, I thought I had. I awakened in the middle of the night and saw a woman's face looking down at me. She was smiling as though she knew me. I didn't see the rest of her body. I didn't want to either. I pulled the bedclothes over my head and trembled until I fell asleep again.

"You were just dreaming," my mother told me afterwards. I was not convinced.

When an old lady who lived with us died, I could not go near her room. I was expecting her ghost to pop up sometime, but it never did. But then I was keeping my eyes closed in the dark! It took another spiritual experience to rid me of the fear but that was some years later. By that time there was more concern about being mugged or otherwise attacked. I was not in the grip of such fears when I was young, even though I had a man try to sexually abuse me in the cinema when I was twelve. No, it was the world of the unknown that caused the fear when I was young. But then, we did have our imaginations stimulated by the cinema. As Snow White ran away from the wicked wiles of her stepmother, trees clawed at her hair and clothes. Later films told us of zombies that roamed and mummies that cursed, and disembodied hands that sought revenge. During the war we had air raids and bombs falling not far away. But I cannot remember being worried about such things. After all, God was on our side – at least, that is what everyone seemed to think.

When I was about ten, Christine, a girl in my class at school, died suddenly with a burst appendix. A friend, who had seen her body, told me that she looked lovely in death. She was dressed in white with a bunch of violets in her hand. I walked past her house with a kind of numinous awe, thinking of her in the front room, seeing her in my mind's eye with those flowers in her hand.

But death was not something that I'd had to face personally. I had a vague idea of heaven because of my Sunday school teaching, but the actual loss, or the possibility of loss, had never hit me until I witnessed my dad having a heart attack.

He was sitting where he always sat, in his big wooden armchair at the kitchen table. Suddenly he gripped his chest and bellowed out in pain. We looked up shocked as he fell to the floor twisting and turning, yelling in agony. I was sent to the front room to sit with our elderly lodger. But I wanted to know what was happening. I could hear the yelling and I was very frightened, so much so that I was crying out in sympathy with my father. I thought he was dying. Someone had gone to the telephone box to ring for the doctor. By the time the doctor arrived, my father was recovering. But it made me realise that nothing was permanent. Even the strong were vulnerable.

I was badly hit when the old lady who lived with us died. Mother went to her room one morning and found her dead. I refused to see her and was almost afraid to pass by her window. During school assembly we were singing a hymn when I suddenly burst into tears. I was almost wailing. It had been a double whammy that morning. Not only had the lady, who had been a sort of grandmother to me, died, but also my name had been read out from the nurse's list of dirty-headed girls. The domestic science teacher took me out into the playground. When I told her about the death at our house, she talked to me about life and death of flowers and plants and how they came up to bloom again. I guess she was telling me that something within us never dies but lives on. I felt comforted, not so much by what she said – as young as I was, I could see flaws in her argument – but because somebody cared enough to talk to me in a kindly, gentle manner. After being bereft and branded that morning, it was exactly what I needed.

Odd things began to happen that increased my sense of awe. There had been some talk of four-leaf clovers being lucky. But I was told there was no such thing. I poked around the clover in our garden knowing I would find one. At each place I looked, one was waiting to be picked. No doubt there is a natural explanation, but being a kid I saw something deeply mysterious about it.

My friend had borrowed my paintbrush. Such things are very valuable when you have very little. Needing it myself, I went to get it back, but no one was at home. In those days doors were not locked, except at night. So I went along to Belinda's room but I had no idea where she had put it. I looked on some shelves fixed to a wall, but no brush. Then I somehow knew where the brush was. I felt quite strange as I slightly pulled the shelves away from the wall. The brush had fallen down the narrow space at the back. There could have been many places all over that very big house where it might have been, but that was the first place I looked. I felt really strange as though I had been given special knowledge. As I left the house I felt I was not alone; unseen eyes were watching me!

Such experiences, and there were many, primed me well for a much later happening. A group of American evangelists visited Nottingham. Being concerned for my father, who had lost the use of his legs, and hearing about the miracles of healing that were supposedly going on, I went along with a friend to see what it was all about.

The church was packed and we had to crowd in the room below. The service was relayed to us and we could hear every word of the preacher. It was highly emotional stuff. A drunken father pressing his little girl's face to a red-hot stove, followed by the story of his redemption through the blood of Jesus. We heard about our sins and prospects for salvation. They didn't sound good. So we repeated the words for forgiveness and claimed our salvation in the name of Jesus.

The next day being Sunday, we visited the church expecting to see pews filled and overflowing. We wanted to hear the testimonies of those who had been healed – or so it was claimed – at the evening meeting. The pews were not filled and there was no healed person there. But one lady was convinced she was getting back her sight; she had seen a vague red at the traffic lights. Everyone praised God. Years later, I was to truly witness God's spirit at work, but it had nothing to do with manipulation and emotionalism.

My mother always said that God helps those who help themselves, and even we kids had done our bit for the war effort. God had answered our prayers by bringing us victory. We now had the National Health Service to bring us health and happiness, and everyone was expecting miracles of that too. But, like my banana, some miracles just cannot be realised!

Chapter Four

Of war and play

By the time I left the isolation hospital, windows were criss-crossed with sticky brown paper but there was little else happening, as far as the war was concerned, in my own little world. The dolls house I had been promised while in hospital was never made. My father was too busy working long hours at the Ordnance Depot. He was also an air-raid warden and would have had the usual practice and patrol work to do in readiness for when the war started in earnest. The Chilwell Ordnance Depot, the local gun factory, the telephone manufacturers, and the nearby Boots pharmaceuticals factory were all to become targets for enemy action.

We were issued with gas masks which had to be carried at all times. Films at cinemas showed people how to use stirrup pumps. They were needed as an immediate aid to combat fires caused by the many incendiary bombs dropped from German planes. We had different kinds of air-raid shelters built. The ones in the park were half buried; the one at our corner was reinforced brick. We rarely left our warm beds to go into the cold shelter; cats and humans tended to use it as a lavatory.

Most of the time, the war seemed far away. We heard about it on the wireless (radio) and saw the news at the cinema. Tanks from the depot shook our house as they roared up the road from the depot, and everything was restricted or rationed, but I was not old enough to know much different.

We moved into our house in Beeston before the war began. It had two reception rooms, three bedrooms, a kitchen we dined and lived in, off which was a pantry with a cold slab (fridges were only for the rich). The bathroom had a rusting bath and was served by furred up pipes, which helped to preserve the five-inch water limit during the war. After the water reached a depth of four inches, our weekly bath was already too cold for comfort. There was a washbasin where I washed my hands and swilled my face. The lavatory had a temperamental pull-chain and an unsavoury seat. This was soon repainted with dire consequences for my sister who sat on it before the paint was dry! There was also an outside lavatory and a rough brick room that housed a coal-fired wash boiler and the coal store. Like most homes there was no central heating. In winter a smelly paraffin heater standing at the bottom of the stairs unintentionally provided heat to melt frost and snow on the roof. It certainly did nothing for us in our bedrooms!

Across the road some houses were being knocked down. We used to sit swinging on the gate (when the landlady didn't catch us) watching the demolition, followed by the building of a cinema on the site. Before long, the red neon sign, *Majestic*, and light streaming out of the glass windows and doors of the foyer, told us entertainment was at hand.

Suddenly the light was no more. Street lamps no longer illuminated our way at night and we had to use torches with pencil beams. Windows had to be blacked out completely so that no light would pass through to guide enemy bombers. Moonlight was magical and stars were like diamonds in the sky - that is, when smog was not blotting out everything around us and clotting our lungs! I was six when the war began. What had been before, soon faded.

Coming out of hospital at the beginning of February 1940 was a new beginning for me. I had been living in a no-man's land, from which the only escape had been in my imagination. Now I was free.

I recall watery winter sunshine and heaped up snow on the edge of pavements. The slush thrown up by passing vehicles splashed my legs and coat with dirty water and compressed snow. But after being in hospital it was fun to be in my home environment for another six weeks, when most children were at school. I was ready to go back but worried that I had a lot of catching up to do. The school I last attended had closed while air-raid shelters were being built, and the infants were sharing another school further away. It was a long, lonely walk. Because of lack of space, children were only getting half time education: one week of mornings followed by a week of afternoons.

My sister was now at junior school and I felt very much alone. Everything seemed so strange. The teacher was pleasant, but by now I had a fear of authority and tended to withdraw into myself. The first morning of our half-day schooling, I just sat at my desk and did as I was told. The last lesson of the morning was arithmetic and we were given two lots of sums to do. I finished the first side of the card and made a start on the second. By this time the bell had rung. Those who had finished their work were allowed to go home. Gradually the children left, leaving me on my own struggling to work out the sums. Tears began to run down my face as panic set in. The list of sums seemed endless. The harder I tried, the slower I got. I would never get home. I was a stupid child who could not do her sums! Seeing my apparent distress, the teacher came over to see how I was getting on. She looked at my work and then at the card.

"Gladys, you are doing tomorrow's sums. You only had to do one side of the card today. Off you go."

Relieved, I went home. But I was feeling even more stupid.

Soon after returning to school, something really dreadful happened, the shame of which was to be with me for a very long time. It was a cold wet day. Playtime, spent in the classroom, was over and it would not be long before it was time to go home. The lavatories were across the other side of the playground – cold smelly places, usually devoid of toilet paper and with brown marks streaked down the walls! There had been no rush to go there during the break. Before long, children were asking to go to the lavatory. At first, permission was given, but after a while the teacher said we must learn to go at the proper time. She sounded very cross.

I needed to go urgently but was afraid to ask. I would just have to hold it until the end of the lesson. I was terrified that I would wet myself. I sat with my legs tight together, utterly miserable. I knew that it was too late to plead with the teacher, I was so uncomfortable that just moving might start the water flowing. I became more and more nervous, and such was the pressure that it was beginning to hurt. I was in agony trying to hold on. The inevitable happened. The warm fluid began to flow into my thick school knickers. Some of it soaked into skirt, socks and shoes, but the rest hit the floor with the sound of splashing water. Alerted, the girl sitting next to me quickly jumped up, afraid of getting wet herself. Gleefully, her hand shot up.

"Please, Miss, Gladys has wet herself!"

There was a shocked silence. All eyes turned towards me and then rested on the tale-tale puddle. Whispers and giggles broke out as the teacher approached the evidence of my dreadful deed.

"Why didn't you ask to go to the lavatory?" she said, with a mixture of anger and incredulity. She turned to my classmate. "Fetch the headmistress, Marjory."

The headmistress arrived. With a look of shocked disbelief on her face, she approached me as I stood in painful distress.

"Why didn't you ask to go to the lavatory?"

"Teacher told us no one else could go"

I stood head down, my face scarlet with shame, as the tell-tale fluid continued to drip from the desk seat onto the floor. My thick knickers were now cool and clinging uncomfortably to my skin, my skirt was wet against my thighs and my socks and shoes were heavy with fluid. The dark stain of liquid told the world that I was a dirty little seven-year-old.

My teacher was not going to accept the blame. "Of course she could have gone. Gladys only had to say it was urgent."

"Never mind," said the headmistress. "Gladys, go and fetch the bucket and mop. In future go at playtime."

My clothes dried on me during the rest of the lesson and on the long walk home.

I lived in fear of my family finding out. Eventually, a child told her elder sister, who passed it on to one my sisters, who then told my mother.

"Our Gladys wet herself at school."

Eyes turned to me. I shrank in my chair. Mother looked puzzled.

"Gladys would never do such a thing."

"It was someone else," I lied.

I felt sick with guilt but I could not let my mother, and the rest of the family, know that I had done something so shameful. She trusted me, and I had let her down badly. I did not want to disappoint my mother, nor did I want to get into more trouble. I would have to live with yet another lie on top of the dreadful shame I was already suffering. As my mother always said: "There's no rest for the wicked."

One day when the school was working afternoons, my mother had to go out to work for most of the day, which meant that I had to see myself off to school. When the time came for me to set off, I couldn't go. I clung to our dog and told her my problem. I allowed tears of self-pity to roll down my cheeks. Jenny licked my face and comforted me. I stayed that way until it was too late to get to school on time. When my mother returned from her work later that afternoon, I gave the excuse that I was not well and so nothing was said. Another lie! More guilt!

But there were happy times at that school. Close by was an abandoned building site. It had lots of partly built walls and a curious flight of steps going downwards for no apparent reason. The children used it as an adventure playground. It became my greatest achievement to leap over the wide space above the steps, defying my fear of falling, and to run along the fairly low walls. I was being no different to the rest of the children. If I was being stupid, so was everyone else!

Within the same area of ground, and elsewhere, there grew sweet flowering nettles. I followed the lead of others and picked the flowers, sucking out the sweet nectar, ignoring the little beetles and ants that ran around inside the flowers. I chewed the young leaves of the hawthorn bushes, which we called bread and cheese. Thankfully, before trying out mushrooms, some concerned person told us they were poisonous. But we picked many blackberries and knew which wild berries not to eat. We even chewed on chunks of pitch, but I wasn't keen. With sweets being rationed and few treats available, we didn't get fat and we kept our teeth!

We had very few books at home. Sometimes I would scan the dictionary looking for naughty words. The only one I remember finding was hospital – it said spit in the middle of it. How shocking! At Christmas we sang carols at school about a virgin. The Salvation Army sang about a virgin; people on the wireless sang about a virgin. What was a virgin? I looked it up. I was none the wiser. It said something about intercourse. I looked intercourse up. Connection by dealings? I was completely baffled. I asked my mother.

"What's a virgin?"

"A woman who hasn't had a baby."

So how could Mary be a virgin mother? Simple. Evidently, God gave her the baby.

Apart from the weekly library book, I did very little reading. We all followed the adventures of Rupert Bear in the Daily Express, and Christmas would not have been Christmas without the Rupert annual. We received Dandy and Beano every week. And later on, Radio Fun and Film Fun broadened our vocabulary. They helped me to read. By matching phrases to pictures, the written word was beginning to communicate in a way that school books had not done, and the comics helped bridge the gap between infant readers and more challenging reading.

My sister Phyllis and I both liked the Alison Uttley books. So when an elderly friend of my parents gave each of us a half crown, we went off to the bookshop. On the way we dropped the money and it rolled down a drain. We looked through the grating and could see one half crown resting on a ledge. We both stood crying bitterly at the loss of our precious money. A lorry stopped next to us. The driver jumped out to ask why we were crying. We pointed to the money in the drain. He dropped to his knees and lifted up the grating. Down went his hand into the filth. First he picked up the coin he could see. Next, he fished around in black smelly sludge until he found the other one. He wiped them both on a rag and then gave them to us. We were overjoyed and thanked him most sincerely. He smiled, returned to his cab and drove off. I can't see it happening today; such a person seen getting out of his cab to talk to children might well come under suspicion.

We knew not to go with strangers but we did not live in fear of them. We had a lot of freedom to play where we wanted. Not far from home there was a little brook flowing between trees where we used to play. We used to call it the dyke. It was murky and muddy. There were no fish but frogs spawned there, and we knew that leeches waited to suck our blood! In the trees there was a little den with a bendy branch to sit on. We would take

some pop and spend some time there. There were a few planks across the brook and I would float sticks to watch them flow under the bridge.

I fell in.

It was like a slow motion film. One moment I was bending over the planks, the next I was looking at the sky through filthy water. Within those seconds I imagined myself covered with bloodsucking leeches and drowning a horrible death. I rose the few inches to the surface, spat out the foul water, and yelled for my mam! I clambered out and ran home.

My mother had just finished washing. The dolly tub was about to be emptied when I turned up soaked to the skin and disgustingly smelly. My mother was furious. After a morning of ponching, scrubbing, boiling, mangling and hanging clothes to dry, she had to start again. She stripped off my wet things and dumped them, and me, in the warm soapy water and gave daughter and clothes a good scrubbing. We were going out that afternoon and I had been wearing my clean clothes.

Poor mother, she had her own private war with a big family of three youngsters and four adults – my dad, my elder brother and two elder sisters – to look after. By the time Jack was in the Air Force and Betty and Barbara were married, Mother had to put up with the temper tantrums of my distraught father as he grew more and more disabled. By that time she was cleaning the cinema to earn much needed housekeeping money.

When I was old enough, I thought about joining the Guides and went to a few meetings. We had to line up and answer questions. The leader asked each person if they had a clean handkerchief. I said that my hanky was always clean (handkerchiefs were boiled white at our house). She smiled and said she meant a spare one for emergencies. I went red and felt very silly – nothing new!

One day we went for an adventure picnic. Rain poured down, I nearly ate the leader's sandwiches by accident, a fire could not be lit, and I was cold and miserable. I did not go to the Guides again.

A year or two later I joined the Girls Life Brigade. We did a little cooking, sewing, craft work, and were offered various useful activities. One night we had young army cadets come to teach us how to read maps. The older girls were giggling and making eyes at the young lads, and that really annoyed me. I thought the boys were rather horrid. One of them was obnoxious and told rude jokes. All they did was flirt with the girls. The boys had masses of teenage pimples, which I thought quite revolting. I had no reason to like cadets anyway. When I was going home one day a group of them dragged me into a garden and forced me to kiss one of them. They all thought it great sport. I was utterly humiliated. After the cadets' visit to the Life Brigade, I was put off going again.

During the war we children liked to do our bit for the war effort. We were asked to collect books and magazines for the troops. We were given army ranks according to the number we collected. I was very enthusiastic. I went from door to door, determined to make it to General. When a cousin called one day with a great pile of education magazines, I was overjoyed. I was about to become a Field Marshal!

To save food crops from destruction, posters were around to tell you to look out for certain beetles and butterflies. We formed a club and got rid of hundreds of them. Unfortunately, pretty butterflies were killed too. I doubt if we made any difference to the availability of food in the shops. Fortunately, we came to see the error of our ways by killing indiscriminately and we gave up the club. We took to watching nature, rather than killing wild life.

Throughout our childhood we had a common stock of games to play. Whips and tops, skipping, and ball games. Some children were quite athletic and liked to perform cartwheels and handstands in the school playground. I was not one of them. We had our playground games, which we played in groups or gangs. *'The farmer in his den'* was one of them. It should have been dell, not den, and we also ended up patting the bone rather than the dog. But then games did not have to make sense to us. *'Poor Mary sits a weeping'*, *'A hunting we will go'*, *'In and out the windows'*, *'There's a little sandy boy sitting all alone'*, were all games we regularly played. No one organised us. We children rounded up those who wanted to play and, before long, others would want to join in. If it was a gang that had got together then intruders were not welcome. Occasionally this led to fighting. I could pull a girl's hair as good as I got!

Skipping was always a favourite game, whether at home or in the playground. Some children had posh ropes, with handles and jingling bells. I was quite happy to get a piece of old washing line. We would count to see how long we could go on for, sometimes doing little hops and various routines to make it harder or more interesting. Sometimes we would skip in two's, or a number of children would skip together, running in and out while two others turned the rope. It could get quite competitive; I won one or two prizes. Sometimes the skipping would be accompanied by rhymes or singing.

Ball games of every kind were played as they are today, but the ordinary little hand ball was in constant use, especially by the girls. Usually we had our dress tucked into our knickers so that we could bounce the ball under a leg before it hit the wall. We would clap in various ways between throws and catches, and all together perform a great variety of movements. Sometimes we would sing to accompany the movements:

"Charlie Chaplain went to France, to teach the ladies how to dance, heel, toe, under we go, heel, toe, under we go."

Hopscotch was another favourite game. Belinda had paving

slabs in their drive, which were just right. The slabs were numbered in the usual way and we would develop complicated ways of hopping and skipping up and down. We usually competed against each other but sometimes we played with others and occasionally formed teams.

If there was one game that brought together children of all ages, it was marbles.

During the war the traditional glass marbles were in short supply and greatly valued. We could buy brown clay marbles as a substitute, but there were glass ones to be won or swapped. We had a great variety of games to play, but children were pretty good at devising their own. The 'wide-boys' of the marble game soon devised ways of increasing their valuable collection.

Objects that cost nothing but gave enormous pleasure were conkers. Once it was discovered that the nuts had reached maturity, the children did not wait for high winds to dislodge them, but rather began an onslaught of heavy sticks and stones. Sometimes more pleasure was found in getting the conkers than playing with them. I felt rich if I had a pocket full of conkers. They were smooth and round to the touch and such a rich colour. I do not recall ever having one that gave me victory but I just liked to have them. They soothe out tensions in the body.

Snobs or jacks were good games, but it was usually boys who played them. We had board games such as draughts, snakes and ladders, and ludo to keep us amused. We used counters from board games and little buttons to play tiddlywinks. Homely paper and pencil games, such as noughts and crosses, hangman, squares, and battleships and cruisers, kept us amused for hours. As we became older we grew in knowledge and that enabled us to compete in making alphabetical lists of flowers, towns, countries, rivers, vegetables, and so on. We also painted, stitched, embroidered and knitted. But when my friend's family bought a game of Monopoly, that really did interest me. Sometimes I was invited to play with them. I thought it quite a privilege to handle the paper money and be given £200 every time I passed go! All our games were simple and without the expense of modern toys. Dolls prams, roller skates and Meccano were the toys to dream about, but new cycles or ice skates were presents for the better off.

But, with few cars and restrictions on petrol, any kind of cycle was a must for those who wanted the convenience of their own transport. Not having a cycle, I always walked or used a bus. So many people used cycles to get to work, there were times of the day when it was impossible to cross the road. You would hear the hooter of the local firm and know that you had about two minutes to get to the shops across the road before columns of cyclists completely blocked your way. No use going to the traffic lights. As soon as one army of men on two wheels came to a halt, another battalion, from a different factory, were already coming round the corner.

I couldn't ride a bicycle and I didn't really want one. I liked dolls but they were expensive. One Christmas I was given a life-size baby doll. It had a china head with eyes that could close. Delighted with my present, I ran next door to show it to an old lady my mum kept an eye on. The ground was icy and over I went. The doll's head was smashed to pieces. I was devastated and ran back home in tears. I knew I would never get another doll. Money was scarce in our family home.

My father told me to collect all the pieces. He spent ages gluing the parts together. To cover the cracks, he repainted the whole head. I could not say so, but I hated that doll afterwards. It no longer looked like a baby. With the hard paint colours my father had used, it looked like an ugly shrunken adult head dipped in chocolate! And yet my father had spent so much time on it. I felt a very ungrateful child. But, when the doll finally came to pieces, I had terrific fun pretending the arms were telephones.

Throughout all my childhood, one thing soon became clear. Women were born to serve men. The men always came first in our house, and probably in most other homes. They never poured out a cup of tea for themselves. They always had the best portions and we girls just went along with it, in fact we helped keep up the tradition. When Bill was younger he had his share of washing-up to do, but I strongly suspect that after the hospital experience Bill had reached the ranks of manhood. When my mother was in hospital I had to take time off school to make sure the chores were done, and the men's meals were cooked and on the table. All I got from them was criticism.

"This cauliflower isn't cooked. I'll get constipation," complained Jack.

"This salt needs drying out," grumbled my dad.

I put the salt cellar in the warm oven and I got: "You'll crack the glass! How did I ever breed such bloody stupid kids!"

My sister didn't escape the whiplash of my dad's tongue. Although she started work at fourteen, she was always helping at home, including assisting Dad with his motor repairs. She made the mistake of swearing in his presence. Men swear; ladies never!

Dad's eyes flashed. "I'll have none of this bloody swearing. If another daughter of mine goes into a factory, I'll bloody cut her throat!"

It was normal for dads to swear. One friend's dad not only swore at his daughters, but slapped them too if they did not behave ladylike.

No doubt, when we played mothers and fathers, we reinforced

all our early training. Likewise our subservient attitude to those in authority. I remember playing school in our garden. I was going round whacking all the dead flowers with a cane.

"You naughty, wicked children," I shouted, as I vented my suppressed anger on anything that got in my way. "Take that! And that! And that!"

Mother always said, "Be sure your sins will find you out." I don't know who I thought was being so very wicked!

A wartime game of who could die the best

Chapter Five

Innocent youth or just plain daft?

My friend Belinda, lived across the road from us. She was the youngest child of a large family. The house they lived in was enormous compared to ours, and they had a very large garden. Once there had been a tennis court with a little pavilion, a kitchen garden with various fruits – raspberries, loganberries, blackcurrants, gooseberries. There were pear and plum trees, and an assortment of apple trees. In the autumn, before going to school, we would search through the grass and weeds looking for sweet apples to take with us to school. There were rose arches and flower borders where beautiful old-fashioned flowers bloomed amongst the weeds. Most of the garden buildings were in a state of decay and much work was needed to restore the garden to its former glory. But it was enough for Belinda's family to cut the grass with their old mower and to grow a few vegetables.

The house seemed like a palace to me. Not only did they have a total of twelve large airy rooms, they also had very good quality furniture in most of them. One of the attic rooms was given to us to play in. Belinda's mother was a real sport and sometimes she allowed us to have a fire in the tiny grate. We would sit close to it on cold dark afternoons and eat the tea provided by her mum. Sometimes we collected beechmast from the tree growing in the front garden. We would carefully peel the tiny nuts and eat them in front of the fire.

In this attic room was a sash window. One day we decided to clean it. My part was to hold Belinda's legs while she sat on the outside sill with her feet dangling in the room – highly dangerous and not to be emulated! We never considered the possibility of an accident. Such things happened only to other people. On another occasion, I held her legs while she dangled over the edge of a canal to collect an arrowhead flower. Neither of us could swim. I guess we were typically crazy kids.

As part of the clean-up session, we decided to scrub the attic floor. I soon realised this was no small task. Concrete flooring is not easy to scrub, and it's very hard to kneel on. I soon gave up the scrubbing and decided to swill my half, but Belinda, being the more patient of us, went on scrubbing. She was exceedingly meticulous about it. It took her all afternoon but she refused to give up. Quite mad. No one was bothered whether the floor was clean or not – certainly not her mother.

The attic became many things to us. As young children it was our playroom. As we grew older it became our sitting room. Then, eventually, it became our theatre.

Acting and dancing began much earlier. When the grass was short enough to play on, the lawn became our stage. On one occasion the grass had not been cut and I ran onto an upturned rake. Painful! So we had to be careful when we took off our shoes. On the grass we would sing and dance. We liked to pretend we were famous film stars, introducing each other to our imaginary audience. "Introducing, Miss Gladys Brock, the famous dancer" or whatever. I would run on to the lawn and take a bow, imagining the applause of the audience. I would do my turn while Belinda was the audience. Then it was her turn. She would do her own thing; prancing around on the grass to music coming from our old wind-up gramophone. So we passed many a happy hour amusing ourselves.

As the war progressed, one of our favourite bits of acting was rather macabre. Belinda's brothers often joined us. We would line up to be shot. The executioner would carefully aim and shoot us one at a time. We would take the imaginary bullet, groan and writhe in agony, fall to the ground, moan some more and finally we would die. The one judged to have died the best was the winner and the next executioner. Since Belinda had two brothers fighting abroad in the war, our game might be thought of as unfeeling. In actual fact such games were probably helping us to come to terms with our hidden fears. But acting was part of our life at that time. We once went to see a film, *Song of Scherezade*, four times, on each occasion sitting in the cinema to see it a second time. We acted it out at Belinda's home until we had it word perfect. We even managed the accent of the French film star, Jean-Pierre Aumont. We bought a record of the music and played it continually.

When we were older we did our little turns at school. Sometimes for school concerts, but mostly in the classroom when the teacher needed to get on with something at the end of term. Yes, we were a crazy pair. The incredible thing is that we were very shy young ladies.

Our attic concerts went on until after the war. By that time I was quite good at sewing and made a few costumes out of old material. We picked flowers from the garden and placed

them over the edges of a mirror laid on the floor. This became a beautiful pool for us to dance around. We had many candles for footlights, but had to take care not to set the house on fire. One day we lit quite a few in a small area. They became so hot they melted into a pool of hot wax with burning wicks floating towards the stage curtain. Not to be recommended! But in those days we did not have the gear that is available today.

Members of both our families became our audience and they were quite appreciative. Once we did a ritual fire-dance, making a fire of battery torches under coloured tissue paper. We danced to the music in our home-made costumes, and threw our magic potions into a bowl lit up from underneath. The potion consisted of liver salts and other things. It came up in a big whoosh, spilling over the top of the bowl. Belinda's nieces were so scared by the climax that they started to cry.

I made myself a ballet dress. I cut my own patterns, so it was

a perfect fit. The bodice material was an old piece of cotton satin which I dyed pink, and the double-tiered matching skirt was made of stiff net. Of course, the skirt was quite see-through but I didn't have enough money for extra layers. We were dancing to the music of the *Nutcracker Suite* and everything seemed to come together. We were very enthusiastic but very, very amateurish. Even so, using a little make-up, and with my dark wavy hair hanging below my shoulders, I thought I looked quite stunning in that dress. I got the impression that Belinda's brother thought so too.

If Belinda's attic was our theatre and her garden our playground, then the riverside was our pleasure park. At Beeston, a canal branched off from the Trent, which at one time would have been busy with barges carrying their cargo to Nottingham. Houseboats were moored along the canal bank and a few craft still went through the lock system.

Sometimes we went fishing with jam jars. Poor fish, they always died. If not by their stay in the jar, then after being housed in the water butt in Belinda's garden. The place where we did our fishing was round the bend, close to the weir. The water was very shallow there and paddling was pleasant and easy. Little sticklebacks and minnows could be seen swimming around, just waiting to be caught with a piece of bread in a jam jar.

Along with the fishing, came our desire to play in sand. Our homes were far from the sea and we did not go on holidays. Day trips were unknown to us and there was no money for such luxuries anyway. By the river there was quite a bit of sand and we decided to take some of it home. We had no idea how much the stuff weighed, especially when damp. We took Belinda's mother's shopping basket to carry it, but the mile-long journey home was hard work for us kids. The handle of the basket broke but Belinda's mother was very understanding about it. We had a sense of achievement, hours of fun, and it cost us nothing.

The river's gravel pits were very inviting. Flowers, bushes and trees grew in abundance around the banks, and rushes grew at the water's edge. Amid all the beauty of plant life, there nested many varieties of birds. Swans, ducks and geese were drawn to the tranquil waters. One day we carried my sister's gramophone all the way there. We thought it would be lovely to hear *Swan Lake* music while we had a picnic tea. But the record didn't sound so good in the open air. The murmur of the breeze through the willows and rushes, the birdsong and all the gentle sounds of a quiet backwater were far more beautiful than anything that we could add to nature.

Picnics were a great pleasure. Once we sat in pouring rain,

one mac over our heads and the other beneath us, while we ate our sandwiches. We watched the swans take off from the water and fly overhead with the distinctive beating of their wings. We found a bird of prey in distress. It had a broken wing and was unable to fly. Avoiding its sharp beak by covering it with one of our coats, we managed to catch it. We took it to the local PDSA, a distance of a few miles, hoping that it could be helped, but they had to put it to sleep. We were told that, being injured, it was very vulnerable and would have met a very nasty death. If we thought about it, birds of prey are not exactly gentle creatures. But we were tender hearted and hated to see any creature suffer. One of the chickens kept by Belinda's mother was badly injured by their cat. The flesh was torn and bones were showing through. I bathed the bird and bandaged it up. To our surprise, it recovered.

Belinda and I took to rowing on the park lake. We always hired a double-oared family boat. Before long we managed quite a good rowing action, in spite of an initial blistered hand reaction. We became exhilarated by our growing aptitude. After spending a number of afternoons of a summer holiday working away to improve our skills, our concentration was interrupted by some youths. They grabbed our boat and tried to tow us. We would have none of it and slapped their hands with one of our oars. They must have thought we were quite mad – two young girls rowing around in a huge family boat. It was pretty obvious they had other things in mind for us. Mad we may have been, but not that stupid!

Our sense of fun could be a bit naughty, if not bizarre. The neighbour who lived in the big house next to Belinda's was a poor lonely soul who tended to drink too much. If I needed a reminder that wealth does not bring happiness it was that poor lady. She liked us to visit and would entertain us by playing her posh piano and singing songs from her childhood.

"Going to school, the cabs at the door...."

We thought this hilarious. But it probably brought back old memories for her. Deep in thought, she was oblivious to what was happening in the present. Before long, her nose would start to run with a thick mucous. It hung from her nose in a slightly swinging motion, getting longer and longer. We would stare at this remarkable phenomenon as it slowly wended its way downward, its pendulum swing getting more and more pronounced.

Would she wipe it across her hand before it touched the ivories? We would mentally put bets on it. Eventually, we would break out into giggles and disturb her reminiscing. But she enjoyed our company.

Belinda had been given a tin of Bournvita that had gone solid. We had this disgusting idea of making it into sweets with a thick pepper filling. Since the neighbour was visiting Belinda's mum, she was to be the first recipient of our joke goodies. They looked good on the plate; quite tasty in fact.

"Would you like one of the sweets we've made?"

"How kind of you," she said, causing me to have a stab of guilt.

But doubts about our trickery soon faded as I watched her put the sweet in her mouth. Biting my lip to control my giggles, I waited for the reaction.

"Mm, how delicious!"

Then came the utter sense of shame. I felt rotten and wanted to confess what we had done. The poor soul had probably lost her taste buds!

It was not difficult to get up to mischief. Belinda's sister had arranged with her friends to have a seance in their dining room. We waited until it was dark, then crept up to a high side window and scratched at the pane with long twigs. It was a few minutes before Belinda's irate sister pounced on us, remonstrating in no uncertain terms about us being bad children. Well, at times, I guess we were. My mother always said the Devil finds work for idle hands to do.

Two highlights of our youth were the end of the war in Europe during May 1945, followed in August by the defeat of Japan. There were street parties attended by whole families. Belinda and I were invited to take part in the victory celebrations taking place in a local street. Food was laid out on long trestle tables with all the families contributing. An effigy of Hitler was fixed to the top of a bonfire. Everybody cheered when it went up in flames. This was followed by lots of family games and competitions. Brenda and I won a skipping competition.

Our own personal effort at celebrating was restricted to making a short string of bunting to put on the front of Belinda's house. Since it was made from drawing paper painted with our paintbox watercolours, it only lasted a few days. But Belinda's family had been pleased to put it up for us, even though it looked a pathetic gesture.

School parties were quite something, considering the large number of children involved. All the children contributed something to eat, plus a paper bag, and the domestic science department did the rest. The party was held in the playground with lots of games. Afterwards, we joined a long queue to receive a bag of food. We had rather a good system of giving presents at that school – good, that is, for those who benefited from it. Each child brought a wrapped gift to be placed in a lucky dip. The prudent thing was to pick out something that felt like a book, otherwise you could end up with a jigsaw with half the pieces missing!

Public celebrations in the park were quite exciting. There were bands playing dance music. By this time we had a large number of Yanks in the area and they tended to lead the way with jitterbugging. One couple in particular caused quite a stir. The man was a tall, well-built American in uniform. His partner, a local girl, was slim and very short. He would swing her around, under and over his body, bounce her on his knee, throw her over his shoulder and twist her around like a rag doll. And all the time their feet would be dancing to the sound of the beat. People would gather in a circle and clap. It was a wonderful thing to join in and be part of it all.

When we were seventeen, Belinda and I went to Prestatyn Holiday Camp for a week's holiday. It was quite an occasion for me as it was my first real holiday. Packing was a time-consuming business in those days. We did not have the easy-care casual clothes that are worn today. Our dresses were packed with tissue paper to stop creasing and, since I had no idea what I might need, I probably took far too much unsuitable clothing. The case felt as though it was full of bricks.

The coach dropped us off outside the holiday camp and we heaved our heavy cases to the reception lounge. After getting our key, we made our way to the chalet that was to be our home for the week. By modern-day standards it was like a hen coop fitted with basic furniture, but from where I was coming from it was home from home.

A walk was organised by the camp staff and we joined the very large group of participating holidaymakers. We were trailing behind right from the beginning. I was used to walking but not up steep hills. It was quite maddening; the group stopped to rest occasionally but as soon as we caught up, the others stood up and set off again. Belinda seemed to be coping but I was continually breathless. The situation was hopeless. We couldn't even stop to appreciate the views. It was just a hard slog. No one cared that we were having a hard time. After a while we were way behind the others so I suggested we take a short cut. Bad mistake – it was a disaster. We finally reached the beach but found ourselves on boggy ground that tended to sink beneath our weight. We were very late getting back, we had mud up to our ankles, and worse – we had missed our lunch!

We had a trip to the Welsh mountains and took a few photographs with the box camera. Of course, everything was in black and white; we had no colour photography in those days, although prints could be tinted. We were impressed by the mountains and valleys, and quite enchanted by the streams and glens. This was all new to us. As new as the rolling sea and surf, the soft warm sand, the rock pools full of little fish, and the dunes that dragged at our feet. In our home town, Beeston, there was a coach firm that advertised holidays. Coach destinations were written on pennants hanging from poles near the local park. Wales was one of the places I'd heard about and longed to see. And there I was, amongst the beauty of it all. I picked some genuine Welsh heather to take home, along with other souvenirs. Little did I realise that one day I would live in sight of mountain scenery and have an abundance of lucky heather on my own doorstep.

At the camp we played tennis on the all-weather courts and splashed around in the swimming pool. In the evenings the camp staff entertained us, or there was a dance organised. Belinda and I were used to dancing together and so we had a jolly time. One night there was a fancy dress party, for which the camp conveniently hired out costumes. The costumes were a bit tatty but it didn't really matter what we were dressed as; the important thing was being there and enjoying ourselves.

We met a couple of young men. The one who partnered me was dark haired and wore very thick glasses. Both men worked in the clothing industry. The morning after the dance, the four of us went for a walk on the beach. I was wearing a very inappropriate woollen suit. But if I looked an idiot, I soon sounded like one too. It was a fair morning and the beach had been swept clean by the morning tide. The sand was firm and smooth under our feet. I looked down and saw what seemed like large flat shells scattered all around in front of us.

"What pretty shells," I said, bending down to pick one up.

They were seagull droppings!

The young men were speechless with embarrassment. We didn't see them again.

The following year we spent a week in London. We stayed with Belinda's sister, quite a few miles from the centre but easy to reach by tube. There was no difficulty in finding our way around; we simply looked at the tube station maps and caught the appropriate trains. We visited the tower and saw the crown jewels, and toured the city to see the major buildings and bridges.

On a visit to the wax works, we looked at the torture exhibition in the basement and I nearly passed out. Seeing a very realistic man in agony, held up by a rope attached to a huge hook through his guts, was just too much. I have always had a strong imagination and that wax dummy was just too realistic for me. I had to get out quick before I lost consciousness.

Starting early in the morning, we took a trip down the Thames to Margate, which was a whole day and evening out. When we returned and left the boat, I suddenly remembered that we had not visited a toilet since leaving Belinda's sister's house at about 6.30 that morning. Fifteen hours of bladder control! How did we do it?

The highlight of the holiday was visiting Belinda's father. He was a civil servant and had a room in the centre of London while he was working on the 1951 Festival of Britain. We found the house where he lived and just turned up. He was exceedingly surprised and quite overjoyed to see us. Although he had a very big family, he had always seemed rather remote. It made me feel good to see another side of him. Perhaps he was a little lonely living in London by himself, or maybe he was so taken aback that we should seek him out.

He insisted on taking us to Battersea Park, which he had a pass for. What a splendid evening we had. Then we met him in the city and he took us to Kew gardens. It was a hot sunny day; so hot that when I sat on a seat heated by the sun's rays, my nose started bleeding very heavily. Belinda's father was quite concerned. That holiday totally changed my perception of the man. He was warm and friendly, generous with both time and money, and not at all the distant authority figure I was used to seeing. I no longer felt myself to be the silly kid from across the road, but a welcomed young lady visitor.

The only thing to spoil the holiday was an unpleasant occurrence on the tube train late one evening. We found ourselves alone in a long carriage with just one other person. The man was drunk and started singing. He started moving in our direction. Belinda remained quite calm. I was getting very concerned but trying not to show it. Past experiences caused alarm bells to ring in my mind. We were getting off at the next station but there was still some way to go. The man had his eye on us and I felt trapped. I had to move away from him. I stood up and moved towards the door but Belinda just sat still. My heart was racing as I waited for the next platform to appear. Would it ever come? At last, after a few minutes that seemed like hours, the train slowed for the next station. The train stopped. Belinda calmly left her seat opposite the drunk and we left the train. I felt really stupid for panicking.

The next year we decided on a trip to the Little Canada Holiday Village on the Isle of Wight. The brochure made the place seem very exciting: log cabins to sleep in, canoeing up a creek, horse-riding in the countryside, fireside sing-songs, trips round the island, dances and much more. It was everything we hoped for.

For the first time in my life, I rode a horse. For some reason I was given the largest mare. Her name was Lady. Someone gave me a cowboy hat to wear and what an odd sight I must have looked in my white tennis shorts and shirt. The horse seemed a long way off the ground and I had difficulty mounting. Someone told me I looked quite at home on the horse, in fact, part of it. I'm not sure whether they were being complimentary or sarcastic. Belinda was wearing jeans and looked quite splendid.

We set off down some country lanes. All was going well until a red sports car came zooming round the bend behind us. My horse insisted on clinging to the middle of the road.

"Bring Lady to the side," shouted the leader.

The horse had a mind of its own. The more I tried to move her in the right direction, the more she slowed and stuck her bum into the middle of the road. The car driver couldn't wait for Lady

to behave; he steered practically into the bushes and scraped past us. Why was I given the awkward mare?

That night there was a sing-song with country dancing around a campfire. Country dancing and square dancing were all the rage at that time. Belinda and I put on our checkered cotton dresses, tied our little scarves around our necks, and went dancing country style.

We met some friendly people and a man asked me if I could lone him a bra and dress! There was to be a fancy dress party the next night and the men were to dress as women. He looked quite good in my clothes but, in spite of washing, the garments never seemed the same after I got them back.

Those post-war years were good and exciting, but the early years with Belinda as my close friend were halcyon days, in spite of the war that occasionally intruded into our lives. I may not have had many clothes or toys, and there were many things that we had to do without, but it was wartime and many people were in the same position. I did not have holidays, but few people did. We had Wakes Week and that was fun. The whole community took part in parades and games. There was no feeling of being poor, at least, not until later years when my dad became disabled and was on sick benefit (a miserly amount compared with what is received today). But we were rich in so many ways, and lack of material riches caused us to feast on simple pleasures.

Good old-fashioned songs were well appreciated (page 76)

Chapter Six

Family affairs

The fact that a fire, no matter how small, was lit every morning in the kitchen for heat and hot water, meant that we always had a lovely warm patch of bricks in the side entrance to the house. Being behind a high side gate, that part of the entrance was a very private place. On the opposite side of the entrance, a close-boarded fence topped by a trellis covered in climbing plants separated our property from our neighbour's yard. During the war, blackout restrictions ensured that the only light at night would be from the moon and stars. On a cold dark night when a couple wanted a little intimacy away from prying eyes, what better place to go?

My lovely sister Betty, and her friendly boyfriend Cliff, must have spent many a happy hour pressed up to that very convenient wall, doing their kissing and cuddling. But it wasn't too long before they married.

After a while they managed to rent a two up, two down, end of terrace house. The front room had a fireplace with a tap to a boiler for hot water, but the shortage of fuel meant that it was rarely used. A bit of furniture and an upright piano filled the room. A door opened to a very tiny front garden. The other downstairs room, the kitchen, had a fireplace with a small oven. The oven had a badly fitted door, which ensured everything cooked in it would be singed on one side. Scorched cakes were delicious! A coal-fuelled boiler was built into the corner of the kitchen for washing clothes, and there was a shallow sink with a cold water tap. Just enough room remained for a table and chairs. Since there was no gas installed or electric sockets, water for tea and washing-up was boiled in a kettle over a Primus stove. A door led the way up steep steps to the two bedrooms. The back door opened on to a shared yard, across which, was their only lavatory. Being next to allotments, the house was plagued with mice and black beetles, as they found out when, on returning home and using the front door, they crunched their way across the floor to switch on the light.

In those days lots of people lived in such conditions. Even after the birth of their two children, and although Cliff had TB badly affecting his one good leg (his other one was half missing due to an accident) they could not get a council house for many years. They were considered to have the basic necessities, that is, a house, and were unable to move up the housing list.

Cliff was a gentle soul. He spent a considerable time in a TB hospital and the diseased hip caused him problems for years. He played the piano very well, which was about the only entertainment they had. Good old-fashioned songs were well appreciated.

"If I could plant a tiny seed of love in the garden of your heart, will it grow to be a great big love some day or will it die and fade away?"

When their son John was born, I used to visit quite often. The baby was only a few months old when I first took him out. Since I was quite young at the time, I was told not to take the baby out of his pram. I decided to go on my familiar walk along the banks of the river. Close to the weir, a grassy ledge lay just below the footpath. It was rather a steep slope to reach it, but I

thought it would be nice to sit and peacefully gaze at the river just a short drop below. I had often sat there with Belinda. Holding tight to the pram handle, I had no problem letting the pram run down. But as I took the strain I realised that it wasn't going to be so easy getting back up. Not to worry, I was a strong girl.

But I did worry. After a while, I decided it was time to go home before John's feed time. I held the pram handle as tight as I could and, with my back to the slope, pulled and pulled, but the pram kept dragging me back to the rather narrow ledge. Should I remove little John, leave him on the grass, take the pram up and go back for him? He was too small to roll about and so fast asleep he wouldn't know he'd been moved. But, engraved in my mind, were the words of my sister: "Don't take him out of his pram."

The alternative was pretty bleak. Getting tired with all the heaving, I might slip and go over the edge. I could envisage me splashing wildly about while John in his pram went floating down the river!

"Can I give you a hand?"

The cavalry had arrived in the nick of time. A young soldier was standing at the top of the rise. He pulled the pram straight up to the path and I breathed a sigh of relief. I did not tell my sister what I had done. I knew I'd been stupid, and I so much wanted to go on looking after little John. If my sister knew that I had once taken the neighbour's baby with me shopping, and being forgetful, had left her in her pram outside a shop on the High Road, she would not have been so trustful in the first place. It would have been no use telling her that I'd eventually remembered and did a record sprint back to retrieve her. The baby had been there for about half an hour!

When John was a toddler I would sometimes baby-sit for his parents. On one occasion I had to give their infant his supper and put him to bed. I had seen it done many times. John always had a mix of cornflakes and warm milk before being put in his cot. How I envied that little lad his soggy cornflakes. I would watch his mother pretend to taste a little of it before spooning the mixture into young John's unappreciative mouth. "A bit for me and a bit for you," she would say to encourage him to eat.

Betty and Cliff went off to the pictures and left me in charge. If that kid didn't want his cornflakes, I knew someone who did!

"A bit for me and a bit for you," I said. But I wasn't going to hang around for ages trying to push it into his tight-lipped mouth. Cornflakes, warm milk and sugar – very tasty!

"Did John eat his supper?" I was asked on my sister's return.

"I did what you did. You know, a bit for me and a bit for you. It all went," I assured her quite truthfully.

I picked up the knack of telling half-truths at a very early age. When I was about four and a half, my mother had to leave me with a next door neighbour while she went to work. I was supposed to be playing with my friend Nora, but her dog scared me into hysterics. I would stand on a broken chair in Nora's

garden screaming my head off, with her barking dog running around and snapping at my feet. It was always the same when I went next door. So I persuaded Nora to play in our garden. She soon became bored and wanted to go home.

"Mummy's left me some salmon sandwiches for my dinner. I'll share them," I told her, hoping to bribe her to stay.

She scoffed down the sandwiches and started off home.

"Mummy's left me a cup of Bovril in the oven," I told her.

She drank the lukewarm liquid and was ready to go.

"There's more salmon in the pantry," I bribed her again.

But this salmon was in a basin and left for my big sister Betty. Betty was a young working girl and came home for her dinners. I gave Nora half of Betty's dinner.

Page 78

Nora went home. Sad and lonely, I waited for Betty to come home.

When Betty fetched her dinner from the pantry she was furious. "You've eaten my dinner!" she accused me angrily.

I truthfully assured her I had done no such thing.

Mother came home and I was accused again.

"Gladys has eaten my salmon!"

"Now tell the truth, Gladys. I won't be cross if you tell me the truth. Did you eat Betty's salmon?"

"No," I said truthfully. "Betty ate it herself."

Well, she had eaten half of it; I hadn't eaten any of it. So it was only a half-truth!

Mother always told us to tell the truth and shame the Devil. I can't say that when I was young I cared much if the Devil was suffering discomfort.

When John was a little older I took him out quite a bit, especially when Cliff was in hospital. Betty had to catch two buses to visit her husband at weekends – she worked during the week – and she would be gone for a whole afternoon. I took my nephew to lots of places and would tell him the names of trees and flowers, and generally give him the benefit of my minute amount of flawed knowledge. I remember giving him a lecture on good behaviour.

"You must always tell the truth and be a good boy. If you are naughty, you will upset your mummy and make her cry."

"Like when she comes home after seeing Daddy?"

My poor sister. Tears came into my eyes. I squeezed John's hand. "Kiss her better," I told him.

I used to take John on the bus to visit a park where there were swings and all sorts of equipment, which are now banned because of poor safety records. On one occasion I had the poor little lad running for the bus with me holding tight to his hand. I ran him into a lamp-post. On another occasion, I bought several pounds of little pears that were being sold off very cheaply. We both ate them greedily. Little John threw up on the swings.

One day, when John was a bit older, I took him to Nottingham

Goose Fair. We used up all the money except for just the amount to get home. John was having a go on the horses but after paying the man, he dropped the change. I was frantic at the thought of walking so many miles home. I could only look for it when the roundabout stopped. It was ages before we got it all back. Giving him the last coin was a stupid thing to do.

On another occasion I took him with me to Nottingham to buy fabric for his mum. When we arrived at the shop my sister's purse was missing from my bag. We didn't have a penny between us. Anxious and angry, I marched in to what I thought was the Police Station but a man in livery stopped us before we got very far.

"You can't come in here," he told me, showing me the door.

"My purse has been stolen," I yelled, trying not to cry.

"Go the Police Station down the road," he told me, moving us out of the door.

John was still hanging on to my hand as we marched down the road. We found the right building and went straight in. I dragged John to the reception desk.

"My purse has been stolen," I told the policeman. "Someone took it from my bag when we were on the bus."

"Perhaps it just fell out of your bag. Give me the details and your name and address."

"I didn't lose it. It was stolen," I insisted.

"You can't be sure of that."

"I can. It couldn't have fallen out. I've got no money. We'll have to walk home."

The thought of dragging my little nephew five or six miles home had sent a tear rolling down my cheek.

"Look, miss," he said, digging his hand into his pocket. "Here's sixpence. Now please give me the details and I'll enter them in my book."

Thanks to the kind policeman we had just enough money to get home, but I had to face my sister and tell her that I had lost her purse, plus all of her money.

On all these occasions, if I'd had the tuppence for the

telephone, there would have been nobody to ring. With no easy back-up from family or friends, we had to learn to be self-reliant. And with no handy phones in our pockets there was less to be stolen.

The Americans were much in evidence in the mid-forties. Many tales would be told of their goings on, especially with the girls. But the Yanks were very generous people. I was with young John outside a pub while his parents were having a drink in the pub garden. A Yank spoke to him.

"Hi, Kid. Would you like a chocolate bar?"

I didn't get one. I guess I was too old for sentimental generosity, and not old enough for bribery with intent!

When winter arrived I made John a sledge. Well, lets say I hammered three bits of wood together. Pleased with my efforts, I dragged the thing to his home. I could see the grin on my sister's face.

"Where are you going to use it?"

That was a good question. We had no hills or even suitable slopes for miles around.

"We'll slide down the side of the air-raid shelter," I said, thinking I was being rather clever.

By the time I'd dragged it the hundred yards or so to the shelter, the runners were distinctly wobbly. One run down the very short slope and I was picking up three pieces of wood. Well, the snow was melting anyway.

When Janet, John's sister, was born, I had another child to dote on. One summer, I stayed at my sister's house overnight. In the morning, while Betty was downstairs getting a cup of tea, I asked if I could get Janet out of her cot. I collected her and sat her on my bed while I slipped off my dressing gown. She folded over like a china doll. I watched it happen but could do nothing about it. Thump! Yell! Screams that brought Betty running up the stairs. Butter was applied to the bump and poor Cliff was told off for not going to his daughter's aid. Since his leg was still hanging up, it was more a case of Cliff receiving shifted guilt. I felt utterly wretched and wondered if I was safe to be with any kid.

My sister Barbara was quite close to Betty. They often went out together, especially before they were both courting. Barbara had a young man, Edwin, who was in the army. I liked him a lot and when he came to our house, I would sing to him, "Soldier, soldier will you marry me, with your musket and fine drum," much to Barbara and Edwin's amusement.

Before Barbara had a chance to marry Edwin, he was sent off to the war and was taken prisoner by the Italians. After he was released and came to visit my sister, I sang to him again but, being older, I was rather shy about it.

He told us stories about the prison camp. The one I hated most was how they would stand ducks on hotplates to see them dance up and down. I was horror-stricken to think that he could be so very cruel. He asked me to come over to him and, of course, I obeyed. He grabbed hold of a tender spot just above my heel and I winced with the stabbing pain. Barbara grinned. "Look, she's going to cry," she said.

Fighting back the tears, I left the room and went to my bedroom to have a good cry. I couldn't believe how he had changed. I was angry with my sister too. She had gone along with his action and laughed at my distress. I put it down to the war and the experiences Edwin must have suffered. The anxious waiting must have been hard for my sister too. Edwin never hurt or humiliated me again. After a while, he seemed much more gentle and was so very kind. I had only just become a teenager, but even then I realised that war does terrible things to the nicest of people.

Barbara's wedding took place soon after Edwin arrived home. Everything needed for the wedding feast was rationed but quite a good spread was organised. A neighbour prepared the salads, arranging them artistically on large serving plates. A baker friend of father's made the cake. Mother and a helper prepared everything else. The wedding reception was held in a large room of The Boat Inn at Beeston Rylands. I helped serve the food.

The cake, when it was cut, was found to be full of ants. It was knocked and banged and the ants were driven from their lunch. The cake was cut and each piece scrutinised before I took the portions to the guests. Edwin's piece was rather small but, since I knew what had been in it, I considered that it was just as well. He smiled at me as I put it in front of him and I felt that somehow I was deceiving him. By choice, I did not have any cake.

My dear sister Phyllis and I would often visit them after their marriage. They lived in the mining town of Kirkby. We had to travel on two buses to get there but Edwin would always reimburse our fares. They were both so very welcoming. I think they enjoyed having us just as much as we enjoyed going. They lived in a prefab. Not a huge place; it was rather like a very large box sectioned into living room, two bedrooms, kitchen and bathroom. It was always very warm in their home. Miners had a generous free coal allowance.

I became quite fond of Edwin and thought him a wonderful person. He had a lousy job working in a pit but he was always cheerful and amazingly generous. Barbara would tease me about my stockings. They were my only pair. They looked all right, but under my skirt and inside my shoes, they were full of ladders and holes. Edwin just grinned at my thrift.

They taught us to play cards and sometimes we went home a little richer. Gambling was part of life in that mining area. But then, my father gambled so it was nothing new to us. Dad would send us off to someone's house to place a bet on a horse. It was illegal and very hush-hush. Later, intent to gain that illusive fortune always beyond his grasp, he would risk some of his benefit money on football pools. One day, I forgot to post off his coupon. It was with fear and trembling that I approached him just after he'd checked his coupon with the football results.

"Have you won anything today, Dad?"

He must have seen my worried face. "Didn't you post the coupon?"

I handed him the envelope. "I'm sorry, I forgot," I said, nearly in tears.

"That's okay. I won't have to get a postal order for next week."

Dad may have wanted his pot of gold, but gambling ten shillings out of his tiny income only made life harder for my mother, and no fortune was worth the terror I was feeling that day.

My dad was quite close to my eldest brother Jack. They had things in common and would talk to each other. They were always cracking jokes, which to me never seemed funny. They were both engineers. They enjoyed a drink at the pub, and both of them smoked. Jack rarely had anything to do with me. He never played with us younger ones, but then neither did my elder sisters when they were at home.

When Jack came home from the Air Force, much to our surprise, he brought a wife with him. I rather liked Peggy, but Mum wasn't too keen. After Jack and Peggy's baby was born, there was a lot of trouble. A full house, poor washing and cooking facilities, the cooking taking place in the room we lived in, made life difficult for Mother especially. Jack would complain about dirty nappies, and Peggy would say there was no hot water. Before long, there was a bust up. Without telling anyone, one day they just cleared off. After a year or two, like a lot of people at that time, they went to Australia to start a new life.

Chapter Seven

I want to be a designer

I felt very grown up when I started studying at the Nottingham College of Art. My dear kind mother had taken me to town to buy me a new blouse and skirt and they looked very smart. I plaited my hair and rolled it around my head. I looked a young woman, rather than a kid, and I felt good about myself.

Among other things, we had life-drawing classes and it was quite something to be confronted with a naked body to draw. I was soon over my embarrassment and concentrated on the job in hand. She was no beauty but we were not there to draw pretty pictures. We were to observe and draw life in the raw: the form, the shadows, the mood.

Before long I was having some of the rough edges smoothed off me – not always gently. In the design class my apron sketches were held up by the lecturer as an example of how not to produce ideas. I never forgot that lesson; from then on my designs were

drawn with light touches of paint rather than with realism. My figures had unnatural nipped-in waists and ridiculous long legs. So much for life-drawing classes, but at least my marks nearly doubled as I began to learn the art of presentation.

Fashion drawing might be ridiculous but clothes had to fit perfectly to the figure and be put together neatly. I thoroughly enjoyed the pattern cutting, and the making-up classes. I was taught many methods of dress-decoration and shown how to use the embroidery machines. The course was geared to what was required by the very many garment manufacturers in the Nottingham area. We also had history of design, and on Saturday morning, lessons in general drawing and painting. I loved every minute I spent at the College of Art and I was doing very well indeed.

Then, after only a term and a half, the enjoyment came to an end. My father's condition worsened and there was no possibility of him ever going back to work. My mother was going out early in the morning to clean the local cinema, and my father was doing his best to earn money from home but, financially, things were very tight. I was sixteen and still in education. The rest of the family had started work at fourteen and I was the only one living off the labours of others. My sister showed me a shop assistant vacancy advertised in a local paper and suggested I start working. So I did.

I was not particularly happy at the shop. I had been told that I would be taught window dressing but it was never mentioned after I started work. I felt rebellious from my first week there. I asked a lady if she would like to try on a deep suspender belt because she was uncertain of the size. The staff whispered to each other and laughed in their hands because only corsets were fitted. I could not see why a small-purchase customer should be treated any different to someone with a lot of money to spend, and felt quite indignant at their mockery.

One day, we had a very long queue leading from the counter, out of the door and into the street. Nylons were on sale and the word had got around. I had told Belinda and her family the nylons were due in that Saturday. I was serving Jean, Belinda's sister, when I found my pencil was missing from the counter.

"Could I borrow your pencil please?" I asked of the shop-owner's wife. "Mine has disappeared."

"No," she said, and went on serving the next customer.

I had no other means of writing and could do no other than stand there looking stupid. Jean was waiting for her nylons, change and receipt. Every purchase had to go through the same process. The pencil was nowhere to be seen, and with the queue getting longer, the situation was ridiculous. People were getting impatient. Humiliated, hot and flushed, I was about to clear off home, when I was given a pencil.

"Make sure you don't lose that one," the woman said in a nasty tone.

That was it, I resolved to move on as soon as I could.

After six weeks of serving in that shop for thirty shillings a week, I had a stroke of luck. Through a friend of the family, who had a relative working as a secretary at a clothing firm, I came to be offered a job as a trainee designer. I was given the opportunity to work my way up through assisting the chief designer and helping out on the cutting benches. When I started work on the factory floor I was just a green kid, sexually inexperienced and socially insecure. I had a lot of growing up to do.

Since the design work was done in seasons, help was not always needed and it was agreed that I should start on the cutting benches and learn that side of the business while waiting to be used by the chief designer.

My first day in the factory was very tiring. The huge building housed jersey-cloth knitting machinery on the top floor, other knitting machinery on the lower floor and the clothing production departments sandwiched in-between. The machinists worked from eight in the morning until late in the afternoon. Machines droned and clattered all day long, except for dinner time when everywhere would go deathly quiet. The noise and the smell of oil and sweaty bodies was quite overwhelming.

It was good to get a morning break. But when I walked into the canteen with the girls from the cutting benches, I received wolf whistles from every male present. My cheeks turned crimson as everyone turned to see the cause of the men's appreciation. I could see them grinning and laughing at my embarrassment. A motherly type went over to the men and told them that I was a lady and did not appreciate that sort of treatment. I was flattered to be marked off as being different from the rest of the girls, but wondered how she had come to that conclusion. In future the men just eyed me up and down but kept quiet.

At dinner time the office girl came to escort me to the canteen. She showed me where to get the cutlery and so on. We sat at a table separate from the workers and ate the first course. She ate her pudding and I watched in dismay. I picked up the spoon and fork she had given me, and sat looking at them. I was out of my depth.

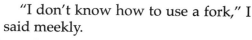

"I don't know how to use a fork," I said meekly.

A look of amazement crept over the office girl's face.

"Well don't use it then."

What a laugh they must have had in the office when she returned. I must have sounded like a five-year-old on her first day at school.

When I arrived home my thumb was sore and blistered from the use of a huge pair of tailors' shears. Garments were cut out from layers of material, as thick as the cutters could manage with shears, so they had given me the job of sorting out

and cutting up waste fabric to break me in. My feet were weary from standing all day and from wearing my new boots that I had bought to ease the chilblains I constantly suffered from. My head was aching from the noise and my mind was in turmoil from the whole experience. The stone

steps, rough flooring, dirty windows and crumbling paintwork were like something from a Dickens' novel; the total lack of what I had expected completely shattered my dreams. As soon as I was home I broke down in tears; I was so unhappy.

I had to pass a gauntlet of wolf-whistling workers outside of an Engineering factory to get to work. Eventually, I found another route – longer but less embarrassing. The fact that I so easily blushed only served to incite men intent on a big tease. The cutting supervisors teased me endlessly. I would be busy working but sense I was being watched. I would look up to see them staring at me. I would instantly colour.

"Why are you blushing, Gladys?" they would mock.

I just had to ride it out. One supervisor was a constant cause of harassment. He would run his thumb knuckle down my spine every time he passed behind me. I hated it. It hurt; it was embarrassing and utterly demeaning. I continually asked him not to do it, but he would just laugh. I felt really aggrieved that he could get away with it. But one day, when I wasn't feeling particularly well, I boiled over. I swung my booted foot at his shin and was pleased to hear him yell.

"You nasty bitch," he muttered, but he never touched me again.

I only earned thirty-five shillings (£1.75) a week and had my bus fares, teas, coffees and dinners to pay for. After keeping a few shillings back for necessities, my poor mother received only ten shillings (50p) a week. But the prospects were good and I was able to save up to buy my own clothes or make them using our ancient sewing machine.

I had been introduced to the senior designer and had seen her office: a simple room with oak desk, chair and cutting bench, and cluttered with rolls of craft paper, fabric and patterns. I saw how she worked. It was obvious she could not draw but that was no problem. All that was needed was the basic design showing details sufficiently for the sample-hand to see how pieces were put together. Since each designer cut her own patterns and gave instruction to each worker of the various processes, beautiful or elegant pictures were not necessary.

I was thoroughly disillusioned. I had expected design studios, where the designers sat in front of drawing boards with pencils, brushes, and everything needed to produce well finished designs to grace the walls of the most elegant of showrooms. But what had I found? Bread and butter designing was more about copying other people's ideas, or at least interpreting them to suit your own customers, and all that was needed were slips of paper and a single pencil. At least it was still necessary to be able to cut a perfect pattern. But I was determined to produce my own original designs – that is, if ever I was given the chance.

Finishing the college design course would have put me straight into a design office, but I had to make it the hard way and the prospects at the beginning were not encouraging.

During that first year of work, I met some very memorable people. Joan, the chief cutter, was a pleasant, friendly person who excelled at her craft. She made the lays (lengths of fabric-width paper perforated with the pattern layout) and cut special samples. She also modelled the new designs for the benefit of the designers and managers. Later, she modelled garments picked out by buyers viewing the new range. Joan was a very confident person and seemed much older than her twenty-one years. She was also an ardent churchgoer. When she knew I hadn't been christened, she was aghast.

"Don't you want to go to heaven when you die?"

I was too shy to tell her, but I thought her religion too simplistic. If all you had to do to reserve a place in heaven was to go through a christening ceremony, then the Christianity Joan believed in was not worth much. I had lived up to then without being christened and I failed to see that "being done" could possibly make any difference to my life in this world or the next.

May, a tall girl of eighteen years, was another cutter. She was fond of heavy make-up: plucking away her eye-brows and replacing them with pencilled arches, plastering her face with foundation and covering it with powder – clouds of the stuff filling the air – and reddening her lips with a thick layer of lipstick. Rouge and mascara completed the finishing touches. Before she applied the make-up, her face was without colour and she looked rather poorly. But May lived up to her name. She was always bright and lively. She did a lot of singing while she worked and she was no slacker. She had a delightful slight lisp as she spoke and she seemed to be always smiling. She was a good friend to me at work and occasionally we went out together.

Now if May used heavy make-up, then Pat must have put hers on with a trowel. Pat was much older than the others but, from a distance, was quite youthful-looking. Her figure was slim and well controlled inside her tight-fitting garments. She wore clothes with high necks or roll collars that overlapped her facial make-up. Her blue eyes, framed with blackened lashes, sparkled beneath carefully plucked and darkened brows and her heavy make-up almost, but not quite, disguised the ageing lines of the face. Her pleasant smile revealed very neat, white teeth. Like the others, she was always friendly and when she asked me one day if I would tell her husband, should he ask, that we had gone out together the evening before, I did not like to refuse. I found out that she was seeing another man and I was not happy about covering up for her. The folk at work knew what was happening and felt sorry for her husband, who evidently was a lovely man, but that did not worry Pat. She would explain that her husband did not have the means to satisfy her. She became a bit of a joke at work.

"Oh, yes. He's always visiting the house when her husband's out. She says it's to fix the television. He just goes upstairs to put up his aerial."

I did not consider it to be an unreasonable excuse for the man to be in her home. After all, television was in its early days and aerials were notoriously fickle pieces of equipment. What I found shocking was that she only ironed the bits of her husband's shirts that could be seen – collar, cuffs and a bit of the front. He seemed to me to be getting short change.

We had a part-time cutter of more mature years but quite an active person. She and her husband went competition dancing. I could just imagine her all dressed up in her many-tiered dresses that she made herself. Sometimes she would get pieces of fabric from the remnant boxes and use them for a variety of sewing projects. She made her husband, and his friend, bathing trunks out of the knitted woollen fabric. She told us what happened. While the men were swimming, the trunks became heavy with sea water. They dropped off and were lost at sea. The women refused to come to their aid with towels, and they had to streak out of the sea and across the beach naked. I believed the story. May had made herself a two-piece swimsuit in the same fabric; the bra drifted away whilst swimming in the river.

There was also a quite elderly lady who helped out occasionally on the cutting benches. She was constantly telling us how good she was at dressmaking and how pleased her clients were with her work. She said her dresses were as neat inside as they were outside. Her cutting was not so brilliant and she was a bit slow. But she thought herself to be perfect. Unfortunately, a car swept her off her feet into the air, causing a number of injuries requiring bones being pinned together. We didn't see her again.

Other people helped out on the cutting bench from time to time. One lady was quite a character. She had a number of children and was clearly pregnant again. They lived in a slum area of Nottingham, not far from the building. She told us quite casually how a rat had bitten the hand of her baby as it lay in his cot. What her children did while she worked, no one knew. I think her unemployed husband was supposed to be looking after them. When asked how she felt about being pregnant after so many children, she just laughed: "Can't do anythin' about it. As soon as 'e 'angs 'is trousers on the bedpost I'm pregnant again!"

Most of the cutters thought her man must have spent most of his life in bed.

For a short while, we had a young man called John supervising the cutters. He spoke very well and was obviously well educated. I knew he lived in a wealthy area between Beeston and Nottingham. He seemed much too posh to be working in such a lowly position. I found out that he was training for management. Much of the time he wore a smart blazer emblazoned with an intricately worked badge. I was curious.

"That's a lovely badge. What is it – a university?" I enquired.

"Rowing club, actually."

"Really? I thought only posh people belonged to that."

He laughed.

I blushed. Stupid me – he was posh!

He designed and made clothes for his girlfriend. It seemed very odd to me. I wondered if his girlfriend became embarrassed when he fitted the dresses. If I'd known more about man-woman relationships I would have known she probably enjoyed it.

Just for a short time, another young man, Roger, assisted John in the cutting department. He was very tall and quite good-looking. At Christmas, the two men bought all the cutters posies of flowers. We were all thrilled by the kind gesture.

"You must let us give you both a kiss," said one of the women.

Kissing Roger seemed like a good idea to me, and no one else was objecting either.

They did not refuse, but rather got us properly organised.

"Right," said John. "We'll go

behind the fabric racks, and you can all queue. We'll both kiss you, but one at a time."

Had they planned it before buying the flowers? But the flowers could not have been a bribe. Looking at us and looking at them, they didn't get much of a bargain.

John kissed me rather nicely. I had to stretch on my toes for Roger to kiss me. Afterwards, I liked him even more and he seemed to like me – or was it my imagination? I thought a lot about him over the Christmas holiday and looked forward to seeing him again.

But on the morning of our return, Roger was missing. He'd been taken ill with polio. We knew we wouldn't see him again. At that period of time, polio was a crippling disease which struck down young people in particular. Many only survived with the help of an iron lung.

The manager of the outerwear department was a lovely gentleman. To someone my age, he seemed to be a bit on the old side. He was quite short, of slim build, had grey hair, and wore glasses for reading. But what I noticed most was his ever-smiling face. He was not easily angered and was generally a very good manager.

I once wrongly costed a piece of embroidery on a suit. I had given a single costing instead of for a dozen garments. A large amount of embroidery was involved–velvet appliqué oak leaves all around the collar and down the front of the jacket. They had already sold a large number of garments before our manager realised the costing was way out. He told me about it, but not angrily. He said that it would have to be made up by spreading the cost out to the other processes. This meant that all concerned would get a little less. The price was corrected for future sales. He was a kind man but no one's fool. He simply knew how to manage without tears.

His deputy was a different person altogether. He could be very unpleasant on his off days. On his good days he was just himself – mildly unpleasant! No doubt he did his work with satisfaction. Whenever the deputy manager came in to the workroom, there was a certain tension. He seldom smiled and was more prone to scowl. It was all change at Christmas. When the girls had been out at lunchtime for a drink, they were ready to kiss the first chap that came through the door. If the manager saw them coming, he would turn and run back to his office, but his deputy seemed to enjoy leaving his office to get kissed.

One middle-aged worker, a buttonholer, was well known for her lack of speed and her fairly casual way of doing things. There was nothing wrong with her work but she certainly lacked enthusiasm. She was the factory union leader so I expect the management would treat her with respect. Since all the machine hands were on piece rates, it was largely up to them how hard they worked. As this lady did the first sample, I expect she made sure that the rate for the job was to her advantage. This was a bit of a ding-dong thing. The management realised doing a single procedure took longer and would cut down the time given. Some of the sample hands knew their time would be cut, so didn't hurry. But generally, things seemed to work out.

The cleaning lady, Madge, was a wonderful person. She had a face and figure the like of which often graced seaside postcards. Her shiny face was oval, her red-rimmed eyes were round and bulging and almost devoid of lashes, her dark hair was dragged back from her face into a net, and when she opened her mouth, stained and broken teeth formed a winning smile. I didn't really

get to know her until I was designing and had my own office. She would come in to clean while I was in there working. I often used to joke with her. Having no friends or family, she led a solitary life. At one time she had been a skilled fabric mender, but being past her best she was given jobs to do that no one else wanted – cleaning all the toilets and offices and doing the rough work in the canteen. Poor woman, she was always receiving complaints about her cleaning skills. I considered her to be unfairly treated and in need of a bit of cheer. My sample-hand and I liked to give her a bit of fun.

"Stand on that mop!" I would demand, and she was daft enough to do it. I would then push the mop over the polished floor around the office while she held on, giggling like a kid.

She was an avid reader of murder stories in the tabloid press, and was always full of the latest reports. Since she had no life of her own, lurid stories were all that added zest to her life. Her landlady developed dementia, accused Madge of stealing and ordered her out of the house. With no one to turn to, she was feeling suicidal before someone at the works found out what had happened. Someone helped her find temporary accommodation, and the firm stored her furniture in their cellars until she needed it again.

I recall my first year at the factory quite well. It was a long hot summer and temperatures rose into the nineties. Joan brought a mobile radio into the workroom so that we could listen to the test matches. It didn't stop us working, and the management made no objection to us listening to the radio – they too wanted to know how England was making out over the Australians. Test matches seemed so different in those days. Everyone seemed to be following the matches and willing England to win.

One very hot day, May persuaded me to take an afternoon off to go rowing on the river. She would automatically get stopped an afternoon's pay and nothing would be said, but I wasn't sure what would happen to me. I was officially staff and did not get paid by the hour as May did. The day was uncomfortably hot. Sweating on the cutting bench was not the ideal occupation for such lovely weather, so it did not take much effort on May's part to get me to go with her.

We took the trolley bus to Trent Bridge and made our way to the rowing boats. We could both row and we took it in turns. While changing over, an oar slipped away and drifted from the boat. It was an anxious time. The current was carrying the oar quickly down-stream. We had to use the other oar and our free hands like paddles. We came very close to falling in the river. After much hard work we retrieved the runaway oar, but we had to work jolly hard to get the boat back in time. May went home and I took the trolley to take me to the bus stop in the town centre. Unfortunately for me, the trolley stopped outside the factory. The manager and his deputy got on and sat almost opposite me. I was a bit late for the bus to Beeston. As soon as the trolley stopped at my getting off point, I quickly jumped off the trolley and ran for my bus. The next morning I was called to the office to explain my absence from work the previous afternoon. I got away with half-truths. I think they'd had a good laugh at my embarrassment.

May really liked a bit of fun and sometimes we would cross our yardsticks. "On guard," we would say, and begin a mock sword fight. It was a bit of a giggle but we had to make sure the management was not around. Apart from wasting time, it did not exactly do the firm's equipment any good.

May and I were invited to a Christmas party at Joan's house. We had a good time and a lot to drink, mostly liqueurs – a new experience for me. I was staying with May overnight and when we returned to her house we had more to drink. May asked me if I would like a pickled onion and when she opened the jar, she spilled them out on to the floor. We ate them complete with fluff off the carpet. I must have had a fair amount of alcohol but it didn't seem to have much effect. May's younger brother had far too much to drink. I saw him turn a greyish green and then rush to the kitchen sink. He was ill for the rest of the night. Well, it certainly stopped me drinking for a while.

Being seventeen was a fairly happy time for me. I was learning about so many things important to my future. After the initial shock of factory life, I soon settled in and was being given the chance to learn more about how designs were created in the factory. I spent a lot of time in the chief designer's office, helping her cut patterns, working out lays and cutting first samples. I was also given the job of grading patterns to different sizes. Eventually I was given the chance to do some designing myself.

A storeroom was cleared out so that I would have room to work. It wasn't much of a place – overcrowded and stuffy to work in – but I soon set about designing what I thought young people would want to buy. I was given the services of an experienced sample-hand who would offer advice if needed, and time the process to the nearest minute. The chief designer vetted my designs to start with, adding or subtracting to fit her knowledge of the buyers' tastes. After a while I was left to get on with it.

It was a great thrill when the buyers came in. I was not present in the showroom, but I soon learned of their interest in my designs when the manager came in with an armful of my numbers hanging over his arm. Only one or two needed altering to suit the customer. I then had the gradings to do for the different sizes and the lays to work out. I was really happy with the work. Unfortunately, when the season finished, I had to go back to the cutting bench, whereas the designers went on trips for inspiration or spent much time experimenting with new fabrics and trimmings. Even so, it was an exciting time. I was seeing my designs mass produced and eventually turning up in local shops and stores. I knew they would be on sale throughout mainland Britain, displayed in shop windows and hanging on rails. Eventually, I passed a woman in the street wearing one of my numbers – a youthful dress with a flared skirt and velvet appliqué flowers seemingly flowing out of a pocket. It was a tremendous boost to my self-confidence.

By the age of eighteen I was about as successful at turning out winning numbers as one of the other designers, even though I had all the other work to do. Since I could sew, I was also a candidate for helping out when machinists were in short supply. After two years, I was only on four pounds a week. No other benefits either. There had to be a better job somewhere.

Chapter Eight

Moving on to where I started!

I responded to an advertisement for an assistant designer in a firm with direct retail contacts. I was to be given £4 10s per week and, along with the rest of the workers and staff, five shillings punctuality bonus and five shillings productivity bonus. The designer was also the manageress, so she had much control over me and my activities. She was a dour, disagreeable person. There was talk that she fancied the boss. She certainly gave that impression when he was around. I couldn't see how she would attract anyone. She was totally lacking in femininity. She was bossier than the boss, and delighted in finding fault. Leave a fine pencil line on the edge of a pattern and she would fetch her shears and carefully slice it off. Since our pencils had to be kept sharpened, the line she cut off was finer than a hair. Nothing less than absolute perfection was good enough. No saving too small. Leave an overhead light on while I made a rare visit to the toilet, and I would receive a reprimand on my return. She gave me hell!

I strongly suspect the woman was sexually frustrated. Apart from anything to do with work, she never had anything to say to me except for little tales concerning male genitalia. Evidently, when a dentist was pulling out one of her strong teeth, she brought her knee up sharply and caught him in his groin. Amusing for her; painful for him! On another occasion she had underpants to make for the boss's dad. Evidently, he complained that the legs were much too short. "I may be short in height, but I've got it where I need it," he told her. In the telling of these stories, she actually giggled.

But why tell me? Did I need to know the father of my boss required shorts reaching almost to his knees? At least, relating the stories brought a smile to her face. With her wide mouth and beautiful teeth, large blue eyes and soft dark hair, she could have been an attractive woman. Unfortunately, although she had a reasonable figure, the way she walked and conducted herself

– like one of Hitler's lieutenants – would put anyone off. That is, unless he or she was a masochist. Maybe the woman had qualities we never saw.

The owner of the firm, who through sheer hard work had built up the business from very little, was quite active at floor level, as well as being its general manager and chief salesman. He had an eye for a good selling line and often brought in dresses for copying. On one occasion he brought in a dress and took it apart himself. The manageress was absent at the time and he wouldn't take me off my important work. He roughly cut out a dress from the pieces and handed it over to be stitched. A proper pattern was cut afterwards. I concluded that the owner's business was partly built on copying fast selling styles that could be done cheaper, a common practice in the rag trade. He also copied dresses he thought attractive and would sell well in fabrics of his choosing. Since I was never consulted on anything to do with design, I have no idea if any of their designs were original.

The boss never took his eye off production levels. On at least one occasion I saw him take off his jacket and assist in the laying up of fabric. He had a business to run and everybody was expected to work just as hard as he did. If a new machinist was behind the rest, no matter how good her work, she would have to go and make room for somebody faster. There were no unions and everyone worked under a two minutes notice-to-quit agreement, whether they realised it or not!

All new patterns were cut in a thirty-six bust size, using a standard basic block altered according to the design. This was important as it ensured that all dresses had a standard fit, and that all patterns graded to different sizes would also have a standard fit. The customers expected all garments to be regular in size and be able to fit perfectly to the body. In those days, corsetry pulled in the waist and shaped and uplifted the bust. Whether there were gathers, drapes, pleats, plunges or godets, the garments showed off the figure to its best advantage. Too bad if one's bits of anatomy did not easily fit into the right mould, but seams could be let out or run in by the alteration-hand that most shops employed.

Most designers had their own basic blocks and guarded them jealously. I had to use the firm's block with no deviation. But I rarely had the chance to cut a pattern from a design. I was kept busy pattern grading, working out economical lays and cutting the first samples. When I had a new pattern to cut it was usually from a dress brought in by the boss. I never did get the chance to produce designs of my own. I had taken a backward step in my career, but at least, I was learning an excellent system of grading.

Before long, I was more frustrated than at my previous firm. True, I earned 25% more money, most of it in bonuses, but there was constant pressure for greater achievement. The girls on the machine bench were expected to keep their earnings at optimum level. There were plenty of women ready to work hard for good rewards and there was no room for slackers. PMT was never heard of when I was young. I knew of one girl who suffered terribly every month but she never had time off, and she kept up the pace in spite of pain and sickness.

The boss never spoke a word to me – not once. Any information was conveyed through my superior, the design manageress. I was once told that someone had applied for a job on the cutting bench, and that he was capable of cutting patterns as well as using the cutting machines. The wage the applicant wanted was much more than I received, but I was told the firm would be better off with him than me. I said nothing but decided to read the job vacancies in the local paper.

When I first joined that firm, it was housed above their showroom. We were packed in like sardines. The place was plagued with mice; one had been known to run up a worker's leg on the inside of her overall. Girls whacked her back to fetch it down! Before long, we moved into different premises on the outskirts of Nottingham. Although an old building, it was a large airy place with plenty of windows to give natural light. But if we opened a window we were assailed by the stink from the glue factory. In summer the smell was nauseating.

We had a nice little canteen with an excellent cook. She produced home-made fare for those who wanted a hot meal.

Girls whacked her back to fetch it down!

Close to the canteen was a toilet. The girls had two lavatories to start with, but were reduced to one when a man started working in the building. Regulations insisted on separate toilets. So he had one to himself while the rest of the workers had to share the other one. At least we had the privilege of a sanitary towel disposer. If you were brave enough to put one inside the contraption, within minutes a smelly smoke choked your lungs. It just could not be made to work properly.

It wasn't all gloom at the factory. We had the radio on during the morning playing the latest hits, and we girls sang along to the music. We all had a bet on how many times our chosen record would be played. I never won a penny.

On Fridays, those who were in during the lunch break bought cream cakes from the near-by corner shop. On one occasion I walked there with a friend to collect the order. We had several paper bags filled with cream horns, vanilla slices and cream sponges. A flock of pigeons flew overhead and splattered us with toppings for the cakes! Laughing, we dusted them over but said nothing. My mother used to say, "Waste not, want not." She also insisted that what the eyes don't see, the heart doesn't grieve!

The highlight of my time spent at that firm came soon after the boss bought his new Daimler. Bearing in mind, the factory was in a rough area, it seemed a rash thing to leave it parked in the side road. We heard from the manageress what happened next. When the boss returned to his car, he found a deep scratch running down the whole of its length. Two little boys were standing by it. He asked them if they knew who had done it.

"We did, mister."

"What with?"

"This," they said, producing a rough rock.

I thought their honesty very touching and their deed quite brilliant.

Before long I found myself another job. I informed the manageress and she was surprised, annoyed and scathing. In her estimation I was privileged to be working where I was. Within ten minutes she had my cards and wages to date, including a week's pay in lieu of the notice I had given. She stood over me while I collected my things, being careful to see what I was taking. Without a chance to say goodbye to anyone, I was escorted off the premises. If anyone left that place, then it was because he or she had been dismissed. I felt like a criminal.

I thought I knew what it was like working in poor conditions, but I had to revise my ideas. My next factory was housed in a very ancient building on the edge of the Lace Market area of Nottingham. Along with the rest of the workers, I worked in a single room with a low beamed ceiling. We had two windows, one of which was by the bench where I worked. The place was gloomy in spite of the machinists' overhead lighting. The atmosphere was claustrophobic, especially on a warm sunny day. The only toilet was on a landing. Torn newspaper served for toilet tissue. The washbasin was also used for washing up cups and mugs, which were usually stacked around the basin.

I was the only designer. I had been accepted on a two weeks' trial basis but I had confidence in my skills. But instead of asking to see my ideas, the boss gave me a catalogue to copy dresses out of. It was not what I had expected. I looked at the blocks for cutting the patterns and found very strange inconsistencies. The back bodice of the thirty-six bust size was larger than the forty bust size! None of the block patterns fitted together well. I made a completely new set to work with. When I asked the sample-hand about patterns fitting at the seams, she said, "They never fit properly. If the bodice is too big for the skirt, we put a dart in. If the skirt is too big for the bodice, we adjust the skirt. We trim off any side seam that is too big."

What a way to work! I made sure every seam would be spot on. I managed to put through ten new samples by Friday afternoon. They looked perfect. The boss called me to his tiny office. The previous designer was with him.

"Gladys, I'm afraid you're not what we're looking for. What we really need is an overlooker rather than a designer. I can't fault your work. If you ever need a reference, I'll be happy to give it. I did say a two weeks' trial. Do you want to stay for the second week?"

I declined and took home one week's pay. The sample-hand told me she was sorry I was leaving.

"We knew you would have to go. You're too good. Mrs Smith isn't going to let any one come after her that's better than she is. You show her up."

I soon got another job. This time I was told I would have to help out on the cutting bench for a while before I could start designing. But I would be staff and I would get my chance once the samples had been put through. I soon found out that even the designer turned out few of her own designs. Brushed nylon was in, and hundreds of tops were being turned out every day. They were little more than copies of popular styles already selling in the shops. I did one design, which was added to the designer's sample rail. Like all the models, it was sold off at the end of the season.

The man overlooking the cutters was far too shy for the job. He appeared to be scared of women. We had some fabric come in that had a nasty bleb running down the centre. It was going to be difficult to cut round it. We sent for George. He looked at a bleb and started to poke at it. When pressed, it kept popping up again. All the women knew what the blebs looked like, and seeing George playing with the things was just too much. They were either smirking or giggling behind his back. He suddenly realised what was causing the mirth and, blushing, made a speedy retreat to his office and sent for the manager to sort it out.

I may not have liked the job but the girls were a good bunch. One of the machinists caused a bit of a stir when she put a dummy's hand in someone's work-basket. A sudden scream rent the air when it was pulled out. But a job is more than a good working environment and pleasant workers. I wanted to design.

Out of the blue I received a reply to a job application I'd made six months before. It was a medium sized firm and I was to be their one designer. I had no competition for the position. I was taken on at six pounds a week with the promise of eight pounds after three months if I proved successful. I couldn't believe my luck.

Things went very well indeed. They manufactured garments for retail as well as wholesale customers. A very large national chain store picked up a number of the designs. It was a great thrill to see them going through the factory in their hundreds and shortly afterwards be on sale at the local store. I met the manager of one clothing store who told me what he was looking for. I produced the goods exactly as he requested.

"Has that little girl really done these?" the manager asked our salesman. I guess I must have looked very young at twenty.

Some of our wholesale clients had well-known designer labels and they were very fussy. They were looking for something special at a very low price. One of them delighted to humiliate. When I was introduced to the lady partner of the firm she gave me a weak handshake and a look of disdain. She picked up each dress in turn and dropped on the floor those she didn't like.

Her male partner asked me how much price reduction they'd get if we left off a bit of the trim. I knew the alteration would cause just as much work, so

I told him the difference would be negligible.

He lips twisted into a sneer. "It must make some difference, ducky!"

Our salesman quickly cut in and told him something could be worked out to their advantage. No doubt he would rather lose some of his commission than miss a sale.

It was a bit of a harrowing experience, but, no matter; they put in a good order.

The factory was on the third floor of a huge building in the centre of Nottingham's Lace Market. I was staggered to see they were still using damp cloths and ancient pressing irons. But they had a good workforce and production was high. Although there was initial resentment from the overlooker who was a friend of the designer who'd got the sack, I had never been so happy at work.

A year later it all came to an end. The owner was taken seriously ill and the business was sold out to a young man who ran a lingerie concern on the top floor. I wrote to the firm where I first worked. I was welcomed back with open arms and was given yet another salary increase. I was then earning more than twice the salary I was receiving when I had left the place less than three years earlier. My sample-hand and a number of machinists from the sold-off business, were taken on too, and we all quickly settled in.

I now had a proper office and was treated with considerable respect. At last, at the age of twenty-one, I had made it. With a year's experience to offer, I was being recognised as a successful fashion designer.

Chapter Nine

Boys!

From an early age I had no reason to like boys. One Sunday, when I was about six, I was watching a group of them digging in a large hole. Evidently they were going fishing and needed worms.

"Come here, little girl, I want to show you something," said one of them, grinning.

Dressed in my nice clean Sunday clothes, I approached their excavation site.

"Come a bit closer."

The group of boys were gathering at the edge of the hole.

"Come on, we've got something for you."

Something for me? What could it be? I went up to them.

"Here, have these!"

I was seized tight. Hands came from all directions. Worms were stuffed in my pockets, up my sleeves, down my neck, in my socks. I screamed and screamed. They whooped with glee.

My sister, who was two streets away, heard my cries and came running. She removed the worms and took me home. I hated worms and I hated boys!

As I grew a little older, one lad would pull my hair just for fun. Boys pulled my friend's plaits. They teased and shouted, and were cruel to God's little creatures. They dissected frogs and were generally obnoxious. One day we caught the blighters poking baby frogs out of a hole in a wall with a stick. We took them on and, no doubt, lost more hair! They shot birds with their air rifles. No creature was safe when boys were around.

The dislike spread to males in general. I heard my mum tell someone about an old man in the park. As he sat on a seat, he tried to hook her ample breasts with his walking stick. When I was twelve, a stranger came and sat next to me in the cinema and put his hand right up my leg as far as my knickers. Utterly shaken, I quickly shifted out of his way. I once had a finger poked between my legs from behind by a man in a crowd. An old man used to sit on a wall and try to touch my growing breasts as I went past. At first I thought it was accidental, but when his hand came out a second time I knew to avoid him. On the way to school in Nottingham, a couple of times I was touched on my breasts as I walked past geriatric men. Males seemed to be obsessed with a desire to touch, handle or fondle! What was the matter with them? Breasts were for feeding babies - even I knew that!

Then it started happening the other way around. One boy asked me if I would hold his willie. I didn't want to touch something he peed out of! Boys were such dirty creatures.

My knowledge of sexual matters was abysmal. Not only was I ignorant of boy-girl sexual relationships, I had no idea that men and women might prefer their own gender. No one had ever told us about homosexuals or lesbians – that was something I learned about when I was in my twenties. Through guesswork, I thought homosexuals were men who touched themselves, and it seemed very harsh to put them in prison for doing such a minor thing. Lesbians, I thought, were actors. I got the name mixed up with thespians.

So I entered puberty totally ignorant about sexual matters. Periods were horrid reminders of a woman's downtrodden lot. Dogs on heat gave me a clue they had something to do with producing babies. If true, the process seemed quite disgusting. Totally unaware of alternatives, we had pieces of old sheets pinned to a piece of elastic for sanitary protection. If changed at school, having to take them home caused considerable anxiety. One day someone broke into my satchel hanging in the cloakroom, and unwrapped my little string-tied parcel. Needless to say, the contents were not stolen.

I remember going to a cinema toilet when I was very young. I saw a slot machine for towels. My goodness but they were cheap! I ran back to my mother who was sitting eating an ice-cream during the interval, and asked her for the money.

"You can get a towel in there for tuppence. Can I get one?"

"No," she said.

"Please, Mum, I'll be able to dry my hands."

"I haven't got tuppence," she said.

How could she possibly turn down such a bargain? I looked at my dad. No use asking him; he was looking the other way and grinning.

I once heard some girls complaining about their feminine lot. Why should only girls have to suffer periods? A know-it-all informed them: "Boys get something much worse."

I often tried to puzzle out what on earth it could be. Can't say I ever saw any boys wearing trousers dripping with blood!

I may have grown up disliking boys, but as my hormones developed I found they had a certain attraction beyond my understanding. Even so, they were not to be trusted.

Ernie was a boy who hung around with a friend of mine called Hazel. We often went to the University Park together. Ernie was seventeen; we were twelve. I suspected I was invited along because Hazel was not allowed out with boys. I was her alibi. We met up with Ernie far away from Hazel's home. They were forever kissing and cuddling and I was just the gooseberry feeling very much left out. Why did he never want to kiss me? What was it like to be kissed by a boy?

Ernie was a proper show-off. He once tried jumping over the park stream. He landed in the water with his feet covered in mud. I was very pleased. What did Hazel see in him? But

I started getting fantasies about him. I would walk down his street, hoping to see him. I hated myself for doing so but I was sort of driven from within. I thought I was in love – just like people in films.

One day Ernie asked me to meet him outside our local cinema. This was even better than his relationship to Hazel. I waited ages for him to arrive, wondering if I should offer to pay for my seat, if he would kiss me afterwards, and if this was the beginning of something big! At last he arrived.

"Hello, Gladys. I want to ask you something."

My heart beat rapidly. "Yes?"

"Has your dad got a propelling pencil?"

"I think so."

"I need one."

The rotter! No cinema, no kiss, no love. And as far as Ernie was concerned, no propelling pencil!

My next male encounter was at school with Jake. Hardly a romance. The boy I actually liked was dark and handsome, but he was the one who'd pulled the chair from under me. The cad!

My first real boyfriend was a lovely lad called Robert. He was dark, handsome with a strong jaw-line, and he had a lovely voice. Being well-spoken, always looking smart and fresh, he obviously came from a good home. He was a young man with ambitions. I actually met him in the dancing class at school. I was amazed when he asked me if we could meet in the summer holidays. A lovely guy like him wanting to take me out! He was brilliant at drawing but wanted to be a curator of a museum. I thought it a bit of a waste.

The first time we went out together was very exciting for me. I bought a new blouse with money borrowed from my eldest brother and borrowed a skirt from my sister-in-law. Robert called for me and we went off on a long walk to King's Mills, near Castle Donnington. Robert was so interesting to talk to; the journey was not wearisome and the time soon passed. I hardly noticed the blisters on my heels. We ate our lunch by the river and I dabbled my sore feet in the cool water. Then we walked back to Castle Donnington and caught a bus home. Altogether, we had walked quite a distance. But in those days we were used to walking long distances. And with pleasant company what could be better?

It was a wonderful summer. Walking with Robert to sites where fossils were found, and seeing inside the rocks he cracked open, was very interesting. We also visited a museum and strolled in the grounds. Under the trees he kissed me. It was quite pleasant. The only thing that spoiled everything was a peeping Tom. He made even simple kissing seem squalid.

At the end of the holiday, Robert went to Technical College and I went to the College of Art and Crafts. We had both started a new life and somehow we drifted apart.

Belinda's much older brother, Arthur, wasn't handsome but he had a smile that curled his lips up at the corners in a most delightful way. His expressive blue-grey eyes were very penetrating, as though he could see my thoughts and feelings. His skin had become a little leathery from years of exposure to the sun, especially when he had been serving as one of Monty's desert rats. His brown hair was already showing a little grey. He was short to medium in height. His body, devoid of any fat, was very wiry. He rolled his own cigarettes – a habit picked up in the army. His breath tended to be tainted with tobacco, but with so many people smoking in those days, including most of my own family, I was used to it. I will always remember him as he often used to sit, curled-up in a chair like a gnome, and giggling like a schoolboy at one of his own subtle jokes. He had a tremendous sense of fun.

It was when we were preparing for a concert in my friend's attic that the little romance between Belinda's brother and me began. I was putting a button on Arthur's jacket. He'd been helping us with the stage curtain. He came to collect his coat. I playfully held it away from him. He then gave me an intense look and said that he would have a kiss instead.

At that time, although I had been to dances with my friend and danced with boys, I'd had very little experience of being kissed. I was not only surprised, I was amazed that a man in his thirties would want to kiss a kid like me. Out of shyness, I ran into the other attic room, but he followed me. He pinned me up against the wall and kissed me hard on the lips. This was a completely new experience for me. Arthur's feelings were somehow communicated to me and left me shaking. He asked me if I could feel his heart beating. I could but it was just the same for me.

Nothing more was said because we heard Belinda coming back up the stairs. I went back to the other room and started sewing again. At least I tried to sew, but I couldn't concentrate.

When Belinda went back downstairs Arthur again put his arms around me and gave me another hard kiss on the lips. He left when Belinda came back up again, and I remained sitting there, trying to control the nervous shaking. I thought that Belinda would hear my heart beating. Surely she must, it was like thunder in my own ears. But she went on chatting and didn't notice a thing.

So that was the beginning of a secret romantic affair that no one ever knew about. Arthur found a number of excuses to get me alone and I must admit I was quite compliant. He'd bought a television – quite a novelty in those days. It was to become a good excuse for getting me alone. On more than one occasion he would say that the aerial needed adjusting and would someone give him a hand in the attic. Well of course, it was always me that went willingly to help. No one else wanted to leave the fireside or the snowy little television screen; they might miss something. But all the action was taking place upstairs!

Once in the attic, the tools were put down and Arthur would kiss me hard. Nothing more; no words, no groping, nothing at all improper. Then he would pick up his tools and we would go downstairs again. The only evidence of what had taken place was the small amount of bruising on my lips but no one ever noticed.

Members of his family were gathered around the television one evening. One of their favourite programmes was on and

their eyes were glued to the screen. Arthur dropped a coin. I helped him look for it. In the semi-darkness, we crawled behind the backs of the television viewers to the other side of the sofa. There we had a kissing session. Such was the power of a tiny television screen to draw attention from all else. Anyway, who would suspect a seasoned war veteran – a man in his thirties – of kissing a girl of sixteen? Not only that, but of doing it just behind where they were sitting?

And so it went on, until one day Arthur tried something that I was not ready for and for which I had a strong sense of taboo. I could not cope with being touched. Early experiences had made all touching seem either dirty or wrong. I pushed him away and froze. He knew the magic had gone, and he never tried to even kiss me again. The private little romance was over and no one ever found out that it had even begun.

A few months later I started work and began evening classes at the Art College. I met a very handsome young man from the Architecture department. He was tall and slim, his eyes were blue and he had wavy blond hair. His voice was soft and cultured. When he smiled he could have been Prince Charming himself. He asked me to go with him for coffee after classes. I couldn't believe my luck.

I met him when classes finished at nine and we went to a café. He bought me coffee and we sat down to talk. Unfortunately I hadn't had anything to eat for about nine hours and my tummy started rumbling. I could do nothing about it. It just got louder and louder. I hoped he would think they were moving furniture upstairs. It was so very embarrassing and I didn't have the nous to laugh and make light of it – such was my ignorance of social niceties. It was incredible how the rumbling went on. It was entirely beyond my control. What was I to do? It must have affected both our moods because he never asked me to coffee with him again. He probably thought I was the sort you couldn't take anywhere without being embarrassed.

Around this time a man at the firm I worked for asked me out. People mocked him and thought he was a homosexual. But I didn't know about that sort of thing, so when they said he was a pansy, I thought they just meant he was rather feminine in his way of talking and walking. Since he was an actor by profession, I thought his funny quirks quite natural. He was about thirty-five to forty, not bad looking although he had a strange way of looking at people.

He seemed to take an interest in me and asked me about my designing. He wanted to see some of my work so I took him some sketches I'd done at home and at the College of Art. He was quite impressed and gave me a critical appraisal. Then he told me I was a rough diamond and needed a little polishing. Would I go out with him?

Now what sort of polishing did he have in mind? Considering the difference in our ages, I said that I would ask my mother. My mother wanted to know what his intentions were, and where he was going to take me. She needn't have worried. I met him one evening on the way to evening class. He stopped me and, just like the Big Bad Wolf, asked where I was going.

"How about coming with me instead? I'll take you to the pictures."

"No thanks. I mustn't miss my class."

"One night won't make any difference."

"It will to me."

He fixed me with a hypnotic gaze. "You know, my dear, the stars are in your eyes tonight," he said in a husky seductive voice.

I wanted to burst out laughing. I must admit I was very flattered but scared stiff as to what he intended doing with me under the stars. I was given a hint.

"Come with me, I'll show you a good time."

"Thanks, but I have to go now," I said politely, trying not to burst my sides with suppressed laughter!

Chapter Ten

You shall go to the ball.

The Nottingham Arts Ball was a big and expensive annual event to be attended in evening or fancy dress. I went for the first time just after starting college. I was sixteen, short of money, and had nothing suitable to wear. So I borrowed a net bridesmaid dress and my dad painted my old red sandals with silver paint. I had to dance with my friend all night. Who else would want to dance with young ladies looking as if they had escaped from a cheap wedding? I looked dreadfully frumpish compared with the bright young things in fashionable clothes or fancy dress. Moreover, the silver rubbed off the sandals, and the buckles made ladders and holes in my stockings.

The following year we went to the Arts Ball again. I had left college but was going to night school. It was at a design, pattern cutting, and making up class that I made myself a really lovely ball dress. I used a pink self-spotted taffeta, trimmed with ruby velvet. I cut it strapless, and boned the bodice to give a good natural shape without the need of a bra. The fabric had not been expensive and economical cutting ensured ten yards would be sufficient. The long skirt was fifteen yards at the hem and it flowed as I walked and danced. My teacher was very pleased with my efforts and insisted on showing the dress off to the rest of the students. Their gasps of admiration did much for my ego, and it was with joyful anticipation that I went to the ball.

What a night! I had a man to partner me for every dance. After dancing with a few different young men, one held on to me. His name was Malcolm. He was a young man doing his National Service in the Air Force and was based about six or seven miles from where I lived.

Malcolm wasn't at all bad looking. But his eyes and mouth were a little too small to make him anyone's heartthrob. He had a pleasant soft Scottish voice, and winning ways to start with, and was to become quite a new experience in boy-girl relationships.

He had come to the ball dressed as a pirate, which might

seem glamorous, but in actual fact his outfit made him look a bit scruffy. But he was being quite sophisticated and not at all shy. I was impressed by his self-confidence. But he was a lousy dancer. I'm not brilliant but if I have a good partner I really shine. With him just making syncopated trotting steps out of time with the music, I nearly tripped over his feet several times. But it was the first time I had gone dancing without having to sit out or dance with a girl. I was enjoying myself and what did it matter if my partner was no Fred Astaire?

He wanted to see me again and I agreed. We met, along with our friends we had gone to the ball with, and went for a walk by the river. It was all very polite and we chatted in a friendly manner. I couldn't always grasp what he was saying because of his accent and it would cause a little irritation on his side, but on the whole we got along fine.

Then he asked me to meet up with him to go dancing. We met another couple; friends of his who were engaged to be married. It was much too early to go to the dance hall and the weather was not fit for walking. It was dark, anyway. So we went to the other girl's house for a while.

It was a nice middle-class home, quite different from my own, and I felt a bit awkward. We had tea and cake and I was asked if I would like to powder my nose.

"I don't use powder," I said like a silly idiot.

It caused roars of laughter. How could anyone be so stupid? With me it was easy! I suddenly realised what I was being asked. I blushed. I went to the bathroom to give my cheeks a chance to cool down. My confidence was getting shaky as I imagined them all laughing behind my back, and Malcolm being asked where on earth he'd picked me up.

Meeting up with others, we finally arrived at the dance hall. We were late and the doors were closed with gates drawn across the porch. No one was being allowed inside unless they had tickets. People were scrambling around and in the midst of it all, I saw Malcolm hand the man quite a few pound notes. We were then allowed to enter. The gates were swiftly closed behind us.

I don't know how we managed to find a table but we did

– up in the balcony. I suspect friends had kept it for them. A pool of money was put on the table and it was continually being replenished. Malcolm, being a heavy drinker, was making sure our glasses were constantly topped up with spirits for him and liqueurs for me.

He seemed bent on just sitting with the lads, telling jokes and generally having a good time. His engaged friend, Larry, ignoring his fiancée who was chatting with others, was giving me his full attention. I rather liked him and thought he was just being polite. But before long, some of the things he was saying, such as how lovely I looked, were getting a bit embarrassing, especially since he was sitting next to his girl.

Before long Larry asked me to dance and I was very pleased to do so. I wasn't used to the sort of evening Malcolm had brought me out to, and I wanted to get away from the drink and cigarette smoke.

There was very little room to dance and Larry held me very close. I was flabbergasted when he started speaking tender words in my ear.

"How can Malcolm ignore you? You're so beautiful. I wouldn't talk to my friends and leave you sitting alone. He's a fool."

What could I say? I wasn't pleased to be ignored while sordid stories and dirty jokes were being told. Of course, Larry was doing something worse than Malcolm's omission but I stayed silent.

"Gladys, you look terrific," he said, breathing hard over my bare shoulders. I was wearing my pink evening dress.

It was nice to be appreciated. But I wasn't used to that sort of thing. We were just moving on the spot and he was holding me tighter and tighter. I wondered if his fiancée was watching. Was she used to him going off with other girls? He stopped shifting about and pulled me up tight against his body. My dress, though low cut, was very well fitted so there wasn't much to see, but he obviously found the view under his nose quite pleasing. His hand reached low on my spine as he pressed me hard against him. "Do you like it?" he whispered.

Did I like what? Dancing? Hardly – we were not even moving! Being with him? It was a new experience being with someone who spoke with passion. Or did he mean being hard up against him? Since there were many layers of dress fabric, plus his suit between us, what could I possibly enjoy? But I gave him the answer he obviously wanted to hear. He seemed pleased.

I just couldn't believe what was happening. A handsome young man I had never met before, in raptures simply because he was holding me tight. Had I, Gladys, really got him going? Or was it my alluring dress that had him all worked up?

When we left the dance floor his fiancée took him over, but he kept his eyes on me. It was getting late and we just sat drinking. My dad would have been horrified.

Malcolm took me home and kissed me. We said our farewells and off he went. At least he was used to walking long distances as part of his forces training.

We went out again; this time to a pub to meet his drinking pals. It was nearly midnight when we took the last bus home. This time Malcolm was more feely-touchy, but he didn't get anywhere. I hope kissing and pressing up to a thick coat was worth his six-mile walk.

We went out a few more times but his drinking put me off and his touching attempts were getting annoying. My lack of response finally dampened his enthusiasm for exploring virgin territory. He went back to Scotland and we soon stopped writing.

My parents were relieved. Drinking and late nights were not what their daughter was used to.

At about that time, my sister told me that a very shy young man she knew wanted desperately to go out with me. Would I meet him? This was something quite new to me; a sort of blind date. I met this young man, Bernard, outside the local cinema. He was tall, had red hair and was quite good-looking. I rather liked him. But his shyness was embarrassing both of us. Not wanting him to think I was expecting the best seats, when he bought the tickets I promptly headed for the door downstairs. Then I noticed he had bought balcony tickets. But he said nothing and neither did I.

We sat at the back, where the usherette had guided us. He produced chocolates and we ate them. After a while he took hold of my hand and held it in his. His palm was a bit damp with him being nervous, but I didn't object. But after a while, the awkward position of my arm was causing pain, so I had to get my hand back for a while. It needed a rest and to dry off! He must have thought I didn't want it held.

At the end of the film we were both too shy to say how we felt. I lived across the road, so there was no need to be escorted home. He grinned nervously when I thanked him. He said goodnight and we parted. We had spoken less than a dozen words all evening.

It had been decidedly nerve-racking. He was afraid of offending me, and I had been trying not to do anything to make him more nervous than he already was. He didn't ask for another date. He told my sister that he thought I didn't like him. He went out with other girls; why should he be different with me? It was very puzzling.

During the summer my French pen pal, Paul, came to stay with us for a few days. He seemed pleasant and friendly. I took him to all the local parks and along the local footpaths. He took every opportunity to kiss and cuddle me. But I hated it. Without warning, he thrust his tongue in my mouth. Since he was a heavy smoker, I found it quite revolting.

One morning, I took him a cup of tea before he got up. He

grabbed me, pulled me onto the bed, and gave me one of his kisses. Ugh! It was disgusting! First thing in the morning his mouth was even staler than the day before. During one of our walks he had me pinned to the ground. He literally tried to get his leg over. It didn't even worry him that people were walking close by. I fought him off. He was quite put out and said that other English girls had let him. Let him what? I didn't ask. I left him in no doubt that this English girl did not do whatever he had in mind. He said that I was an actress, putting on a big act.

You would have thought that Paul had got the message by then, but no. After we returned from a dance that night, he had a go at seducing me in the kitchen. I was wearing my strapless evening dress and I didn't want him near me. But as I made my way towards the door, he switched off the light. I switched it on again. Before long, the light was off and he had me on the floor. My mother must have heard the noise and called out for me to let him get to bed as he had a train to catch in the morning. I must have been a great disappointment to him. He returned to France and we did not correspond again.

There was a young man that I really did fancy. I was eighteen and ready for a little romance in my life. I was working as an assistant designer at the time, and had been asked to man the firm's stand at a major exhibition put on in Nottingham. One of the firm's new designs had been cut to my size, so I could truly represent the firm. Either that or they thought my clothes not good enough!

A very handsome young man was on the stand opposite me and we had little chats in slack periods. His firm manufactured lace and he gave me a few exquisite samples for personal use. At the end of the week there was to be a huge fireworks display in Wollaton Park. It was familiar ground to me and I was pleased to meet him and show him how to get there on the bus.

It was a magnificent evening. The trees in the gardens and avenues had been strung with lights, and fireworks lit up the sky in cascades of light and colour as we walked the paths and enjoyed the sweet late summer evening.

"This is really lovely," he said, his face a picture of happiness.

"Archie in wonderland," I said smiling.

He gave a little laugh. "That's right. Wonderland!"

We didn't hold hands or anything, but I felt very close to him. It was a warm, friendly relationship. We liked each other. He insisted on making sure I reached home safely, and so we both caught the bus to Beeston, my home town. The bus was to make a return journey to Nottingham – the last one of the day – and I insisted he stay on it. If he couldn't get a taxi he would have had a very long walk. But how I wanted him to take me to my door; who knows where things might have gone from there? I never saw him again.

We had a lovely young man called Barry working at the same firm. He would often use the edge of my long, wide bench to sort out trimmings. The manageress told him off for doing so.

"Move from there. You're disturbing Gladys," she told him.

"No he's not. We aren't even talking!" I told her.

"You don't have to talk. I can see he's distracting you."

That woman hated anything that might cause me to slacken pace. She would even time me if I went to the lavatory.

All the girls loved Barry. He was tall, athletic, fair and handsome. We got on very well together. He bought himself a chest expander. While the manageress was out for lunch, he showed me how it worked – stretching it to develop his chest and arm muscles.

"You have a go," he said, handing the thing to me.

I started pulling. It was tough going. I soon gave up. Not because of the effort needed, but because I realised I was unwittingly showing of the fullness of my breasts. How embarrassing!

"Not bad for a girl," he said.

Red faced, I hurried back to work.

He left the firm just before I did.

"Well, I must clear up, darling," he said, as he was packing away his things. He put his hand to his mouth. "Did you hear that? I called you darling."

"Yes, now you're leaving," I joked

He looked at me, smiling sort of tenderly. Was he going to ask me out? No. Another good one got away!

I met Les at the square-dancing night at the Nottingham Palais. We formed a partnership for dancing. He was a lovely lad and we got on very well. Like Joan, some time earlier, he wanted to save my soul by getting me to a church font. But he gave me a 1662 Prayer Book to see what was involved. I was rather touched that a boy was after saving my soul rather than molesting my body. Although Les would have liked to take our relationship down a romantic road to marriage – in those days, there was no other respectable alternative – it was definitely not on as far as I was concerned. I had already met the love of my life and there could never be another man for me.

I met my future husband on the morning bus. As I had to get off the bus quickly to catch a trolley, I would sit on one of the long seats near the door. He would sit opposite me. He couldn't take his eyes off me. It was getting embarrassing. As far as I was concerned, he looked pretty scruffy and he was always fidgeting as though he was wearing a hair shirt. But I found him very attractive and his voice was so strong and pleasant. Eventually, he sat next to me and we talked about things in general. Then he asked me to go with him to the pictures. It was nice to see him in a suit for a change. After the cinema, he walked me home. To my surprise he kissed me. Our first date and he actually kissed me! He just lifted my chin and softly touched my lips with his own. That was it; my fate was sealed. We had nothing in common; he was a typical male chauvinist. I knew he would use me as a doormat, but I loved him. And fifty-one years later, I still do!

Conclusion

The beginning of the new

I was married in 1953, the year of the Queen Elizabeth's coronation and the beginning of a new era. But people were still more concerned with the marriage, the coming together of two people in a lifetime commitment, than with the actual wedding. We spent only what we had saved. Borrowing was difficult and debt almost a disgrace. We lived according to our means. I made my wedding dress and the material cost me just £2.10s (£2.50). The two bridesmaids' dresses cost me £2 to make. We hired a room and did our own catering. Cake and flowers were bought and a taxi to take me to the church was hired. We bought the basic furniture and lived in a bed-sit for three years. We managed to get a mortgage to buy a house. We had no central heating, no washer, no fridge, no vacuum cleaner, no telephone, no television and, other than the mortgage, no debts!

Our nearest telephone was two streets away and it still resided in a big red box!

The cake was full of ants (page 83)

CW00429522

Not much m
BUT WE DID
HAVE FUN

AGNES SKYRME

White Tree
Books

First published in 1993
by White Tree Books
an imprint of
Redcliffe Press Ltd
49 Park Street, Bristol

© *Miss Agnes Skyrme*

ISBN 1 872971 79 2

Dedicated to the villagers of Westbury-on-Trym past, present and future.

Acknowledgements: Rosemary and Ernie Walker, Audrey V. Smith, Sheila Kotak, Barbara Doré, Mary Maberley, Dorothy Howard, Margaret Bird, for without their help this book would not have seen the light of day.

British Cataloguing-in-Publication Data.
A catalogue record for this book is
available from the British Library.

Typeset and printed
by The Longdunn Press Ltd, Bristol.

PART ONE

THOSE WERE THE DAYS

Part One
Those Were The Days

Preface   5
Those Were The Days   7
Westbury Bound   11
It's All Change Down At The Coffee Tavern   13
Down Our End   16
The Postman's Christmas Breakfast   19
The Village Blackboard   20
Polly Has A Brush With The Law   21
The Black Maria   22
1914   23
No Need For The Town Crier   25
The Day The Armistice Was Signed   27
The Unveiling Of The War Memorial   30
Street Games   31
Growing Up In The Village   32
The Little Room Behind The Shop   39
Mother's Pride   42
The Boy Cousin   43
Hot Cross Buns   44
'But That's Before My Mother Was Born!'   46
Aunt Sarah Jane Is Coming To Tea   47
The Move   50
The Wedding Of The Year   51

4

On Our Mantlepiece Stood A Most Imposing Looking Clock

On our mantlepiece stood a most imposing marble looking clock.

'Isn't it beautiful,' said our visitor. 'I bet it's heavy.'

'It is rather,' said my mum. 'Try and lift it.'

Our guest moved towards the fireplace, raised her arms and tensed her muscles. The family watched with bated breath.

She shrieked as her arms flew upwards. My father made a grab for the clock, for it was made of tin, and had been filled with Chlorodine Lozenges. (These containers were a perk for the shopkeepers.)

As the laughter rang around the little room behind the shop, mum wiped the tears from her eyes and exclaimed.

'We haven't much money BUT WE DO HAVE FUN.'

'What gave you the idea to write your book?' asked the long legged, mini skirted, charming young reporter from Radio Bristol. She was referring to my book, The A.B.C. of Westbury Village. The Butcher, the Baker, the Candlestick Maker.

WELL!!!

ONE
Those Were The Days

Those were the days my friend
We thought they'd never end.

The same names were seen over the shops for year after year.

Families staying put for generation after generation.

'Close knit community' were not just a few words that slipped easily off the tongue, for we were just that.

Horses were still shod in the High Street, bread baked on the premises. Housewives ran to the door, jug in hand, upon hearing the cry, 'milko, milko,' as the milkman and his horse and cart gently plodded down the street.

Girls played hopscotch in the street and boys rolled marbles in the gutter.

Of course, we had our squabbles and fall-outs, our ups and downs, but we lived through two world wars, survived the General Strike and the years of the depression, even thrived on the meagre rations, never heard any one say, 'I must go on a diet.'

Mothers, as ever, coped heroically with the traumas of epidemics before the benefits of antibiotics and the N.H.S., many sadly watching their little ones die or left crippled for life.

Nurse Mizen, Westbury's own Florence Nightingale, worked endlessly, night and day, caring for the sick, the needy and the elderly. For many years her only means of transport was her old, trusty bicycle.

Nurse Mizen, Westbury's well-loved District Nurse with the young ones, at Agnes' birthday party. Rene Mogford (Wiltshire), Gladys Rowley, Phil Bailey, Jean Lee and Betty Davis. Can you guess where this was taken?

All this time the white cat with the pink eyes lay luxuriously stretching or sleeping on the chaise-longue in Butt's shop window, amidst the dust and cobwebs.

Change moves in slippered feet, so we hardly noticed when a shop changed hands, when the old farmhouse was razed to the ground, with houses built on its surrounding fields and the new roads named, Westbury Court, Fraley, Falcondale, Canford Road, Merlin Close and Cooper Road.

We did notice when the drinking fountain was removed to Canford Park, for the war memorial took its place. When the wraps were removed, we watched our elders read the names carved in stone on that tall edifice, but why, oh why, were the men blowing their noses so hard, and why were our mums dabbing their eyes when they didn't have a cold?

Years later, we understood they were remembering those boys and men who once, like us, happy and carefree, roamed the fields and woods, paddled in the Trym and dashed up and down the roads and streets, in that part of the 'sceptred isle' that we are proud to call our 'Village'.

It was quite a night when the last tram came to Westbury. We all trooped up to sing 'Auld Lang Syne' and wave a fond farewell. We watched as the tram lines were removed and thought it was progress!

The gentry left their stately homes, and the houses became institutions.

The little cottages that huddled together in small alleyways all around the village were thought not suitable for human habitation and condemned. The families who had raised their young and lived in cosy neighbourliness were packed off to the new housing estates.

'We may have a flush lavatory,' said one, 'but I wish I was back.'

The little chapel at the bottom of Chock Lane, or rather in Trym Road, became the Labour Exchange.

Our Police Station ceased to be a Police Station.

When hostilities ceased in 1945 and we had time to pause and take stock, with almost a sense of awe we realized how lucky (or perhaps blessed would be a better word) we had been, for all those places we held most dear were left unscathed. Whatever religious persuasion we followed, our own special place of worship was left still standing four square and intact.

The old college had once more withstood the onslaught on her ancient portals. The men's club was ready with open arms to welcome back its old members and to open its doors to a new generation.

Now this just leaves one more important Westbury landmark, the building on the top of the hill, which has cast a benign eye over the village for many a decade.

Its war weary subjects had failed to notice that, like an elderly Victorian lady who has known better days, she was slowly drifting into genteel decay. Like Sleeping Beauty she quietly awaited the arrival of her rescuers.

It was a long wait, until 1972 in fact, before a new breed of villagers climbed the hill and stormed the ramparts, spearheaded by Frank Richards and his merry, but hard working, band of lads and lasses not waving swords and pistols but armed with paint pots and brushes and other tools of the trade.

After years of hard slog our Village Hall is restored to even greater

9

beauty and usefulness. Once again the rafters ring with laughter and the sound of music echoes in the air as the 'old girl' opens her doors and, with arms outstretched, welcomes yet another generation of Westbury villagers.

So with these good folk, and the Westbury-on-Trym Society plus the churches, united as never before, and other activities, the Mothers Union and Townswomen's Guild, my generation can see that our old village is in safe hands and will sail proudly and successfully into the twenty-first century with all flags flying.

TWO

Circa 1885

Westbury Bound

'Where is this Westbury-on-Trym?' asked my country grandmother of the eldest of her five sons, as she supervised the packing of his belongings.

'It's a village in Gloucestershire,' was his reply. He was leaving home for the first time and looking forward to finding fame and fortune (both escaped him), but he did evoke envy, if not fame, when he bought a penny farthing bike. Alas, envy soon turned to ridicule; riding down Henbury Hill, yet to be macadamed, the front wheel struck a stone, and he was flung into the air, landing on the top of the high wall which ran from top to bottom, whilst his machine went sailing on. The raucous laughter of his friends was to echo in his ears for many a day. Why, oh why, is there always someone around to witness our disasters?

Meanwhile, in another part of Somerset, my other grandparents were getting ready to accompany their daughter on the long walk to Minehead Station, for she was going to visit her aunt, who had also 'emigrated' to this village in Gloucestershire. She kept a shop called the Coffee Tavern, situated opposite The White Lion, and within hailing distance of the old college and Parish Church. Thus it was that my parents were introduced to each other in the very shop which was to bear the name 'Skyrme' over its portals from 1909–1975.

Those of you who now live in the village and its surroundings, would be hard put to imagine the village of those days, for even when I was growing up there was no Falcondale Road and its Cote offshoots, no Priorys, no Pinewood, Cote Lea, or Grange Park, no Northovers, Westovers, Eastovers or Southovers, no Hillsdon, Southdown, Shipley or many others. It was a jewel set in a sea of green pastures.

The wedding of Arthur and Polly took place on November 22nd 1894 at the Parish Church. Afterwards they and their guests drove in style, in horse drawn carriages hired from Wallbridges, whose livery

11

stables were in Stoke Lane, next to the men's club.

They were heading for Cheriton Place, where the reception was to be held in the little house which was to become their first home. The carriages progressed down the narrow Henleaze Road, for they took the long way home, and in places the brambles of the blackberry bushes stretched right across the road and met in the middle and had to be switched back by the coachman's whip. Much water has flowed, trickled or rushed down the Trym, passing under the road only yards from our shop on its way to the channel, and eventually to the sea.

Almost one hundred years have passed since that happy day. What changes we have witnessed, what events, and the advance of modern technology beyond our wildest dreams and imagination.

How shopping habits have changed. The loss of childhood innocence is a matter of regret. How sad that they have to be warned about so many things.

As we pored over our school books, struggled with 1066 and all that, and coped with the trauma of growing up, we little thought that we, too, were living in history and that many of those events now would be part of the school curriculum. In eighty odd years I have never lived more than a mile from the shop over which I was born, and I might well have lived there to this day if I hadn't been 'shopped' over a 16 ounce blown tin of baked beans and by a customer too! But that is another story. Enough, enough, for time is fleeting and I must get a move on if I am to record memories of those early years, some very precious, some humorous, some poignant and some written with tongue in cheek, which my kindred spirits will appreciate.

1904 was a momentous year in our village history, for it was the year that big brother, or is it sister, the other side of the Downs, stretched out its ever greedy fingers and plucked that little Gloucestershire village to its ample bosom. The little jewel that we know as Westbury-on-Trym was incorporated into the teeming, bustling City and County of Bristol.

THREE
The Year of 1909
It's All Change Down At The Coffee Tavern

There was going to be a wedding in the village. Nothing earth shattering about that, but the event was to be the link that shaped the future lives of three girls yet to be born.

For the bride lived at the Coffee Tavern, the little shop opposite The White Lion, down at the bottom of the village, and she was going to wed Harry, the youngest son of the retired widow, who had kept the butchers which overlooked the river Trym on the other side of the road.

Thus it was as high summer gently changed into the misty days of autumn that it was all change down at the Coffee Tavern. My great aunt Bess's only child was being married, and her mother decided that it was a good time for herself to retire.

'How about you taking over the shop?' she said to her niece Polly. My mum jumped at the chance. It was just the opportunity she was seeking to put into practice all the skills she had acquired during training under the strict supervision of the Victorian cooks. She was a brilliant cook and knew all about handling money, for she had to account for every halfpenny spent to the lady of the house.

I suppose in this day and age these skills would be classed as Household Management and Business Studies. It was with light feet and joyful anticipation that Polly tripped down the hill from her home in Cheriton Place to say, 'Yes, yes, please, please, we would love to take over the shop.'

'Good,' said her aunt, 'but I'm afraid a snag has cropped up. Mrs Phillips, the shop owner [who also traded down at the bottom of the village] has decided to sell the premises.' Polly's face fell.

'Oh dear,' she sighed, for she could see her dream slipping away.

'Ah,' said aunt Bess, 'but your Uncle [John Symons' father] and I have talked it over and we will lend you the money. You can take your

13

time in paying us back.'

The purchase price asked would seem ludicrous, compared with today's, for my great niece's wedding dress cost more than that which her great grandparents paid for the little shop and its living quarters. It was a long time ago, and the first week's takings were one pound ten shillings (£1.50).

October 13th 1909 was moving in day, and a week later, on the 20th, Harry and Florence, the boy and girl who were born and lived in the village for the whole of their lives, took their vows in the Parish Church, a marriage which lasted well over fifty years. I know, because I went to the Golden Wedding party.

Polly rolled up her sleeves and set to, to build up the business, first to pay off the loan, and then to make enough so that her spouse, who had kept his job as a baker, could join her in their little enterprise. However, according to the gossips, another snag cropped up, me. My parents were reconciled to the idea that their son, now aged 9½ years, would be an only child, but fate ordained otherwise. I arrived on the Westbury scene on June 14th 1910.

Looking back, it was quite a prolific time in the village, for sons and daughters were born to the 'Butcher, the Baker and the Candlestick Maker' and many others, all of whom helped make up the little community of Westbury-on-Trym. Some followed in their parents' footsteps and carried on the family business into the next generation, thus ensuring that the same names remained over the shops for many a year. Many became my closest friends and lifelong companions, none more so than the little girl born to the jewellers up the road on St. Valentine's Day, 1910, and the two daughters of the girl who once lived down at the Coffee Tavern and who married her sweetheart, the widow's son, who lived just over the road.

So the scene is set, for all these characters will people the pages of the book I am about to begin, plus the ever faithful Dorothy, who joined our family in 1924, and in this Year of Grace 1993 is still with me, and Dorothy Sims, our childhood confidante, our friend, our memory jogger.

'How much?!' she gasps when told the present price of an everyday item. 'Remember when we sold soda for one and a half pence for two pounds and then put it in a bag.'

I sometimes greet her, 'Well, and how's my old friend Dorothy?'

'Mustn't grumble,' she sighs, but then she is approaching her 98th birthday. She then pipes up with a twinkle in her old, tired eyes, 'Dorothy means "A Gift from God" you know.' I do know, for I have had three Dorothys in my life. To put it another way, they were all gifts to me.

'Don't make your life sound too like Utopia,' I was advised. Of course it wasn't. I, as well as everyone else, had my share of ups and downs, but so, in spite of being dubbed a 'Pollyanna', I shall chiefly record the funny hours. It was a surprise and a delight to receive so many letters saying how much 'You' enjoyed my first book, *The ABC of Westbury Village*, and the memories it evoked. But the ones that gave me most satisfaction were the ones which ended,

'But above all it was such fun.
It made me laugh.'

On the way to Canford Park for Mary Long's birthday party, with Wally Long her cousin, and Dorothy and Gladys Rowley.

FOUR

Down Our End

As you stand in line at the Post Office it will be hard for you to imagine that on this very site was what we knew as 'Cooper's Barton', the farmyard of the Westbury Court. The entrance was just off the village High Street and facing Church Road, where a flock, albeit of a different kind, can still be seen wending its way to worship at the ancient Parish Church of the Holy Trinity.

A high stone wall, which marked the boundary of the land known as Church Fields, was demolished and a rank of shops built on the site. This wall, and the Westbury Court Farm across the way, had the effect of almost dividing the village in two.

As the twentieth century loomed, it was 'up top' that the village began to expand. A rank of shops, which included three banks and the Post Office, were erected in the grounds of Cambridge House. Just around the corner in Cambridge Road (now Crescent), the tiny library was to be found, where only books were borrowed, and where we children were expected to walk on tiptoe and speak in whispers . . . or else!

Number 38 Westbury Hill was brought into use as Westbury's very own telephone exchange, and it was most appropriate that the prestige number, 'Telephone Westbury 1' was allotted to one of the village's favourite sons, Mogfords. Two more assets were the drinking fountain, now replaced by the war memorial, and the tram terminus. Nevertheless, we, down at the bottom end, had many of the personalities one associates with a country village.

I have already written about my friends on the right side of the village in my book *The ABC of Westbury Village*, so let's cross over, take a stroll down the High Street, and meet the folk who lived and worked on the other side. What a motley crowd we were. Next to the new Post Office are the red bricked villas, erected by the well-known and respected Harris family. They lived at number 41, which was no doubt custom built, for they had quite a large space behind to house all the equipment necessary for stocking their trade. It was a good

16

place for us kids to mooch around while our mothers took tea, and handy for other young nippers to creep up and skip over to scrounge apples from Coopers' orchard just over the wall.

Harry Edwards lived and conducted his newspaper business from number 47. He was a familiar figure, shuffling around the village, wearing a flat cap and peering through thick pebbled glasses. Next came the Police Station. In one of the little cottages, which lay hidden behind the blacksmiths, lived the character known as 'Old Devon', the fresh fish man, who carried his wares around the village in a wicker basket covered with a white cloth, which the customer moved aside to choose her fancied piece of seafood.

How many villages could boast a farrier right in the middle of its High Street? We had two, William Mealing and Jimmy Grigg, living and working almost cheek by jowl, both well-known and respected members of the community.

So it was natural to see and hear the steady plod of the farm horse, a high stepping hunter or the dainty trotting pony drawing a Governess cart, on its way to have a pedicure at one or the other of these gentlemen's establishments.

A leaking tap or a burst pipe, then Mr Walters was your man. An urgent call for help was answered immediately, but otherwise it was a laconic, 'Be up in the marnin ma'am.'

'Oh Lord!' said my aunt, 'That's the third time I've heard that.' For life moved at a slower and gentler pace in those days.

In the High Street lived Mr Alexander the chimney sweep, a most important member of any village community, especially at spring cleaning time, when housewives clamoured for his services. In so much that he often had to start at 5 a.m., he was a man of his word and always on time. Many a flustered customer in reply to his knock had to dash downstairs to let him in. He was affectionately known as Alec, and was often requested to greet the bride and groom on their wedding day, for he was not only a clean sweep but a lucky one.

To liven up the left-overs or a bit of bread and cheese, folk made their way to Linterns. For two pence pickled onions or piccalilli would be ladled into the customer's basin from the two large glass jars that always took pride of place on the counter.

Next came Drew's Stores of blessed memory. The Granary came next. The chuff chuff of the machines as they separated the chaff from the grain mingled with the clang clang sounds of the anvils further up the road now seem sweet music to the ears, as compared to that of the

17

noisy motor car of today.

We now pass over the Trym. This side and just around the corner were the two shoemakers, Mrs Anstee's dairy, which I have already spoken about in more detail elsewhere, and we were at number 1 Passage Road. I wonder if we, at that time, could be classed as a Sports' Equipment Distributor, for among the stock my parents paid for when they took over the shop, were marbles at 10 a penny, tops and whips, penny whistles and pea shooters.

At number 3, Wilfy Lintern operated as a barber, one penny for a shave and two pence for a haircut.

Mr William Davis was a baker at number 5. His bakehouse was at the top of Watkins Yard, while across the road was the White Lion Hostelry. I warned you that we were a motley crowd, and I think you may agree. Another plus, up Trym Road, which is now The Villager, Mrs Wright was renowned for her faggots and peas, a tasty nourishing meal for the princely sum of sixpence ($2\frac{1}{2}$p).

The smell of freshly baked bread and of those faggots and peas, and of burning hooves, mingled with the sound of the anvil, the heavy or light tread of horse power, of the farm animals being driven up or down the High Street on their way either to or from the market, all went to make up the sights, sweet smells, or whiffs, and sounds of a country village in the early part of the twentieth century.

Only two names now remain from my growing up days, the two 'Big Ms', Mogfords and Mealings, and they have obligingly situated themselves one up top and one down our end, so honours are even.

To diversify is the 'in' word at the moment, but Mealings did just that many decades ago, as they turned swords into ploughshares.

The motor car replaced the horse and the village gradually changed from rural to urban.

Wrought iron candelabra is just one of the many lines Mealings now produce, so although many of the family shops, including the butcher and the baker, have left the village scene, we do now have a candlestick maker.

FIVE

The Postman's Christmas Breakfast

'Sorry I'm late,' said the young Mabel, 'but Father Christmas has been.'

My mother, Polly, looked up with a smile for, although it was only 5.30 a.m. on a crisp Christmas morning, she was already busy laying the long trestle table in our living room behind the shop in readiness for the village postmen's Christmas breakfast.

Out in the kitchen, bacon, sausages and black pudding were piled high, plus a dish of local farm eggs and loaves of bread baked at Sims, the bakery just across the road, awaited the time when the tired but cheerful men were expected to arrive after finishing delivery of the Christmas mail.

After filling her children's pillow cases, my mother took one of young Mabel's thick black woollen stockings and proceeded to fill it with a few nuts, an orange, an apple, and pink and white sugar mice and other Christmas baubles, plus a handkerchief, a pair of gloves, hair ribbons and such like. Unfortunately the sticky dates had lost their wrapper and lodged in the toe of her woolly stocking. So Mabel had to fish out another pair, not easy with only the light of a candle, hence her tardy appearance.

My brother and I were told to stay upstairs and play with our toys, but we couldn't resist creeping down and peering around the heavy curtains, which used to cut off the draught.

What a merry scene met our eyes, a roaring open fire, the tantalising aroma of an English breakfast, the happy banter tossed one to the other, as the men tucked in, with the knowledge that a good job had been completed. Ernie and Eddie Drake, Mr Iles, Arthur Smith and many others. Can anyone else come up with a few more names?

As I write this in 1993 the young Mabel is in her 95th year, and we still have a giggle about her Christmas stocking.

19

SIX

The Village Blackboard

'I see Ellings have got their board up,' said my mother. 'One of you nip over and see who's died.' For it was a village custom that when a member of the community died, shopkeepers would erect a board to announce the death. A black-edged card would be attached giving details and the more important the personage, the wider the black edge and the more fulsome the message of condolence. Little groups of people would gather around and chat as they peered up to read all about it. Then the news would spread like wildfire around the village—more effective and cheaper than buying a paper.

I suppose the board would be a flooring plank, cut to fit the shop window from top to bottom, then painted black. Our board doubled up as a shelf to stand bottles of sweets on, covered with crêpe paper, the colour of which depended on the season, red for Christmas and green depicting spring. When someone died the board was hastily retrieved, dusted down, and, if necessary, given a fresh lick of paint. No way would Polly have a shabby board on her shop front—so disrespectful Someone would be hurriedly despatched up to Fearns, the newsagent, to buy a card, and thus all would be ready for Dad, hammer in hand, to complete the job.

I don't know when this custom ended, probably during the First World War, when death, alas, was an all too frequent visitor in every corner of our dear land. Names that would have found a place on the board in many years to come can now be seen, and much too early, carved in stone on that tall edifice which stands where the drinking fountain once stood.

SEVEN

Polly Has A Brush With The Law

'A penny bar of chocolate,' asked the young lad.

'Sorry,' said my mum, 'it's after hours and I'm not allowed to serve you.'

The disconsolate youngster shuffled out of the shop.

'Mrs Skyrme!' thundered a voice. As if by magic, a figure in blue appeared in the doorway.

'You know,' continued the voice, 'you are not allowed to sell chocolate after eight o'clock.'

'I haven't,' replied an indignant Polly. 'Go and ask the boy – he's only across the road.'

'Um!!' snorted the policeman, and went on his way, thinking another chance missed of getting his sergeant's stripes.

'Blinking upstart,' said my father (for evidently he was not a local Bobby). 'I reckon that one's looking for promotion.'

It was the time of the Defence of the Realm Act, known as DORA. You could sell a quarter of ham or a half pound of sausages – they were considered perishables, for refrigerators were yet to become part and parcel of a shop, let alone a home. I don't think we had one until after the Second World War. In fact I know we didn't. When Ellings over the way had a whole side room turned into a refrigerator to store the meat, it almost became the Eighth Wonder of the World.

It is almost impossible to contemplate what shattering effect it would have had on world affairs, let alone on our family, if my mum had been found guilty of selling a penny bar of Fry's Five Boys chocolate after hours. It may have changed the whole history of the world.

The only names of policemen that spring to mind are P.C.s Bob Evans, Bridgeman, Joby Gouch, Padfield. Can any of you come up with more?

EIGHT

The Black Maria

Even television, with its ability to bring news and events instantly into the home from any part of the world, can eventually pall. Then it's a case of 'just another war', 'another shooting', 'another murder'. 'Oh, turn the knob and let's lose ourselves in the fantasy world of the soap opera.' But living in a small village at the turn of the century, even the smallest diversion was something to savour, and the sighting of the 'Black Maria' was one of them.

The Black Maria was the van used to bring a prisoner to the Police Station. The building is still in the High Street, but no longer used for that purpose. The crime committed was probably one of 'being found drunk under a hedge', 'poaching a rabbit', 'fighting outside the White Lion', but certainly not for breaking the speed limit; unless a horse galloping full pelt up the village, or a squealing pig escaping from the slaughter-house and making a dash for it, could be considered dangerous.

Someone calling out 'The Black Maria's up the road,' was enough for people to stop, stare and crane their necks, for anyone rushing up to get a better view would get short shrift from the local Bobby. You can be sure there would be no sign of a mass of reporters milling round, microphones at the ready, unless 'Windy', our very own local reporter, had the good fortune to be passing by at the time.

When a female prisoner was held overnight my great aunt Beth, who had the shop before us and must have been the forerunner of the modern day woman police officer, was asked to go up and frisk the poor unfortunate woman.

Great aunt Beth also had the 'franchise' for providing the prisoner's supper. This consisted of a hunk of bread and cheese and a billy-can of tea, for which service she was paid the princely sum of sixpence. My mother was to carry on this practice later, and when I was considered responsible enough, about ten years of age, I had the privilege of taking up the prisoner's supper.

Privilege indeed, for although I was friendly with the daughter of the Chief Fire Officer, whose living quarters were behind the station, I deemed it most unseemly to be seen going into a Police Station and crept up the road, fervently hoping that no one I knew would spot me carrying out this which, I thought, a most demeaning task.

But isn't it interesting that the things that caused us so much anguish when we were young are the very memories that make us roar with laughter in the years to come.

NINE

1914

Never such innocence
Never before or since
As changed itself to past
Without a word – the men
Leaving the gardens tidy,
The thousands of marriages
Lasting a little while longer:
Never such innocence again.
                    Philip Larkin

It was when I reached the line of the verse 'The men leaving the gardens tidy' that I suddenly became a child again. I was a little girl, walking hand in hand down Henbury Hill with my dad from his allotment, which nestled just over the wall between Sandy Lane and the main road.

As we entered our shop, he greeted my mother. 'Polly, I've planted the beans. Let the boy [my brother Arthur] keep an eye on them and stake them when he thinks it's time; the canes are in the hut.'

At the age of 47, my father had received his 'calling up' papers, and was about to leave to serve 'King and Country'.

23

As I walked a little way up Chock Lane with him, for he was to report to Horfield Barracks, I pleaded with him, 'Oh, why must you go?'

'Because, my dear,' he said, 'this wretched war has already taken the cream of our nation, and now it is up to us who are left to go and do our bit.'

'But don't worry,' he continued, 'I shall soon be home on "leaf",' the term used by the 'Tommy Atkins' for their leave. (Tommy Atkins was the name given to the ordinary man who was conscripted, as opposed to the Regulars.)

'Never such innocence', yes I think this a very apt title, when comparing those times with the lives of today's children.

Many years later, I was standing chatting to a group of friends.

'Weren't we innocent?' said my friend, Val, laughingly.

A more 'worldly' friend, overhearing the conversation, snorted, 'You weren't innocent, you were ignorant.'

However, whether innocent, naive, or just plain ignorant, one thing I do know, our childhood lasted that much longer than that of today's children. They have to be warned about so many things, but we were able to roam the woods and fields or play our games of make believe without a care in the world except, 'Oh gosh, is that the time. Mum said I had to be home by four. Goodbye. See you tomorrow.'

TEN

No Need For The Town Crier

Nowadays, folk with grievances can write letters to the papers, discuss them on the radio, or even appear on television; but in our village the natives had a much more subtle approach. They would stand, if not on the housetops, at least on their doorsteps, and scream about any complaints or wrongs, imagined or otherwise, that had befallen them – maybe about the neighbours, the other children, or the local shopkeepers. I can remember at least two occasions that we came under fire.

About a quarter of a mile from the shop, lived a family which consisted of a wife, a dog and a husband, and believe me, that was the precise pecking order! She was a formidable lady of ample proportions, ruddy complexioned, with a mop of frizzy black hair. One day she could be heard yelling her head off, complaining that she had been overcharged down at the shop. On her next visit Polly asked, 'And what was that all about?'

'Oh, I made a mistake. It was all right when I looked again.'

'Well, in that case you had better go back and shout again, hadn't you?' said Polly.

Victor, her rusty black Pomeranian, was a bad-tempered, yappy old thing, but I must admit that even he had his uses. His mistress would ask anyone who chanced to be passing to hand into the shop a note requesting – no, rather demanding – that her order be sent up at once. Sometimes the shop would be busy and her order overlooked. When that happened 'she who must be obeyed' would jam her hat over her bit of frizz and set forth to come down and do battle, preceded by Victor, barking like mad.

'Gosh, that's Victor,' someone would exclaim, and in those few seconds of reprieve, her few items would hastily be put together and a dash made for the door. When the two forces met, one would gasp.

'Just coming, just coming,' and the other, with a sniff, would mutter,

'Mmm, Mmm'.

Phew! What a relief, for once again we had been saved by Victor's early warning system. Bravo Victor.

Another time she came in for half a pound of tomatoes. She had first walked across the Downs, down Blackboy Hill, and scrutinised the shop windows of Bendalls, David Greig, Home & Colonial, the Maypole and the rest, only to discover that our tomatoes were still a penny a pound cheaper, so then she walked all the way back, just to save a halfpenny.

'And I wonder how much shoe leather she wore out!' Polly murmured as the good lady left the shop.

On yet another occasion a mother with a family of five mischievous kids could be heard shouting for all and sundry to hear that 'her down at the shop had tried to poison them by putting soda in with the sugar.'

'Oh, whatever next,' sighed Polly.

Sometimes there would be a much more poignant occasion. During the First World War, all too frequently the telegraph boy would deliver one of those dreaded yellow envelopes containing the news that a loved one had been killed, or was missing on the Western Front. At these times a great wailing would issue from the doorstep. Cottage doors would open, heads would appear, and the wailing cease. The woman, with tears streaming down her face, would mutely hold up the envelope and neighbours would rush over. Some came to gawp, some to console, but the oldest and most understanding one would place her arms around the trembling shoulders and whisper, 'Come inside dearie, let's make a cup of tea.' I wonder if this sort of thing happened in other parts, or was it unique to our village?

ELEVEN

The Day The Armistice Was Signed

You will know it as The Ridgeway, but to me it was the entrance to the little farmhouse where my cousins lived. Large iron gates straddled the road, which was wide, but little more than a farm track. 'Trespassers will be prosecuted' said the sign, for the land was owned by Sir Thomas Lennard, the Boot and Shoe Shop magnate. That didn't include me, for I was family, and I probably cocked a snook as I swaggered by.

On this particular day Dorothy, the elder of my two cousins, and I were clearing out the fallen leaves from what we called the moat, in front of the house. The house stood quite alone, surrounded by fields and woods as far as the eye could see. A large garden ran down the back, almost to the present Northover Road.

In the field in front we made hay, watched the sheep shearing and played with Lily, the pet lamb, who always appeared at the sound of our voices.

If there was an air of expectancy around on this particular morning, we were unaware of it, for we little knew that this day would become one of the most momentous dates in history.

We heard a voice shouting and paused from our labours. In the distance we saw a figure we knew. It was Minnie, my mother's help, waving a stick with her red tammy shanter tied onto it.

'Peace is signed, peace is signed,' she cried, her face even redder than her hat, caused by the effort of running up from the village to bring the news. For the date was November 11th 1918, and it was on the 'eleventh hour' that the actual signing of the Armistice took place.

When the news filtered through to Westbury that now it was official, and all fighting was to cease, my mother sent Minnie (for few people had the telephone) post-haste up to the farm to pass on the good news to her cousins.

Dorothy (Sims), our much older cousin who was staying at the farm, and my aunt exclaimed 'Wonderful news, wonderful news,' flung their arms around each other, and the tears streamed down their faces. We youngsters looked on in amazement; fancy crying when you said you were happy. Never did understand grown-ups!

We went to resume our playing, but oh no. I was hauled into the kitchen, my hands and face washed, and hair tidied, a penny thrust into my hand, and, 'Now you go down to Aunty Pobs' shop and get a penny packet of Symingtons dried pea soup.' All through the weary years of the war, the two women declared, 'We will have pea soup for dinner the day peace is declared.' Now that day had arrived and the pledge simply had to be kept. I didn't think much of having to leave my play. I was only eight, and my cousins six and three years old.

Can you imagine my journey? No paths, no Eastover, Falcondale Road, Whytes Close or Shipley Road, but fields all the way until I reached the little cottages above our shop.

Years later, Wally Woodsford, the chauffeur at Henbury House, came into the shop and asked for a packet of the same soup powder.

'Charge it on Mrs Gunn's account,' he said, and in an aside to my father, he said, 'Got a leak in the radiator. This is just the job for stopping it.'

Ugh! No wonder we didn't much like our so-called Armistice Day treat.

However, all work at the farm stopped. George Henry, the odd job man, declared,

'Ain't going to do any more today.'

'Fair enough,' said the farmer.

PEACE IS SIGNED

'Fill up your bottle; there's a cask of cider in the shed.'

After dinner, best coats and hats on, we all trooped down to Taylors in the village to buy our Union Jacks and then back to the shop and upstairs. The balcony at Buckingham Palace had nothing to compare with our window that overlooked the White Lion. Can you imagine the jockeying for position that went on.

Down below there were people milling around, singing and dancing. People looked up and waved to us and we waved back, but some stayed behind curtained windows with just their memories.

Dusk began to fall, time for the party to break up, as the little family wearily trudged home and along the unmade path, now Ridgeway, with little Gladdie asleep in her pram. Hearing the sound of snoring, the two women peered over the wall to behold George Henry, fast asleep, a beatific smile on his face, and clutched to his bosom an empty cider bottle.

'Give him a poke,' said my aunt, 'or he will catch his death of cold.'

King George V issued a decree that for evermore at the 11th hour of the 11th day of the 11th month the nation would come to a halt, all activity would cease. For just two minutes every one of his subjects would stand and silently remember all those who had died for their country and those that still suffered to bring peace to the world. As the church clocks struck the eleventh hour machines were switched off, traffic came to a standstill, drivers got out of their vehicles, removed hats and bowed their heads. The milkman held his horses and did likewise, and the baker stopped kneading his dough. Whether farmer, shopkeeper, customer or children at their desks, it was the same. Up the road the sound of the anvil was stilled as the smithy, hammer in hand, joined with his fellow men.

It was most impressive, but life has to move on, and it was not practical to continue in the same way, so now we remember on the first Sunday nearest to November 11th, when, still, the villagers gather at the war memorial in the High Street.

TWELVE

The Unveiling Of The War Memorial
Sunday, July 11th, 1920

Sunday dawned bright and sunny. This was the day the memorial was to be unveiled.

Soon after one o'clock my cousins, Dorothy and Gladys, arrived, dressed in their Sunday best; straw hats on, complete with elastic under the chin. Later, three excited little girls and their parents made their way up the village.

There seemed to be hundreds of people milling around, and we waited eagerly for the processions to appear from Canford Park. We were most impressed by the dignitaries – the Bishop, the Lord Mayor, the Clergy and the choirs. We listened to the service and joined in the singing. A hush fell as the bugler sounded the 'last post'. The processions left, the crowds broke up, and three solemn little girls wended their way down the village.

I pondered the words of a hymn I had heard my mother sing:

> Time like an ever rolling stream
> Bears all her sons away;
> They lie, forgotten as a dream

I thought of all those brave soldiers and sailors being swept down the Trym and forgotten. I felt so sad. I had a funny feeling in my throat and a prickling behind the eye. Tears up to now were only ones of frustration – not being allowed out to play, or being sent to bed before we were ready.

'Was it,' I ask, 'was it a child's first awareness of the sorrows of the world?'

THIRTEEN
Street Games

As in every other village of the British Isles, Westbury had its seasonal street games. I don't remember the correct order, but hopscotch, marbles, whips and tops, hoops, skipping ropes and conkers all duly appeared at the appropriate moment.

In the shop we sold marbles at 10 a penny, a little more for the special fancy ones. Tops and whips were also sold – whips with string for the beginners and very posh whips with leather thongs for the big show-off boys.

In the cold season, boys would have empty cocoa tins with holes pierced in them and then filled with smouldering rags. They would chase around holding these to keep their hands warm.

Hoop races would be held – up Trym Road, down Church Road, around the drinking fountain, and back down the village.

I wistfully watched the girls playing hopscotch; they appeared so skilled in my eyes, but they were a very close knit crowd, and anyone a little different would not be invited to join them. I didn't go to their school, and my mother kept a shop. She had probably stopped credit for one of the families, so I was regarded as a blackleg and not invited to join the 'play union'. However, they did relent and let me try skipping – they must have known it wasn't one of my better talents!

Skipping rhymes went: Tinker, tailor, soldier, sailor, Rich man, poor man, beggarman, thief, and Silk, satin, muslin, rags.

Well, I always managed to get out at beggerman and rags, which was rather worrying, but was it, I wonder on reflection, 'sabotage', so I withdrew and let them get on with it.

FOURTEEN

Growing Up In The Village

The war had ended, the Belgian refugees, who had been housed in the college (the part on which now stands Westminster Court) now returned to their homeland. I still remember two of the little girls, Bertha and Marianna.

The dreaded yellow telegrams, informing the families that yet another Westbury father or lad had been killed on the western front, had ceased to arrive.

My mum used to send parcels containing a bar of chocolate, a fourpenny packet of Woodbines and some home-made cake to each soldier. We received a card addressed to 'Mrs Skyrme, The Lollypop Shop, Westbury-on-Trym.' His message read, 'Thanks for the parcel, I had a dip in the briney coming over, but all's well.' We learned later that his ship had been torpedoed in the channel. (This was Lena Newman's uncle, Reggie Yates.)

Life resumed at a gentle pace for us children. Looking back, I realise we were cushioned from the harshness of the world and I suppose we were very naive, but our childhood lasted that much longer.

I was talking to a young friend, aged six years, who was telling me about her pregnant cat – the only time I came across the word pregnant was when I was quite a bit older than her and had managed to smuggle my mother's *Woman's World* up to my bedroom for a forbidden read and saw, 'there was a pregnant silence'! Sadly, the children of today have to be warned about so many things and their childhood is soon left behind them.

There were so many colourful characters in the village. Banana Joe, pushing his red and white cart, with its flat top stacked with bananas at two a penny. The rag-and-bone man gave away paper windmills in exchange for a jam jar. The Hurdy-Gurdy man, with the monkey on his shoulder, played happy music and the girls would come out and sing or dance around the Barrel Organ.

Another character now missing from the village scene was the night watchman in his little hut, the fire in his brazier giving a cheerful glow in the village street. This time it was the boys who gathered around, to sniff longingly as he cooked his fry-up, and maybe allowed them to roast a potato in the fire and listen to his yarns.

The errand boys whistled the latest songs as they cycled by delivering the goods – remember the age of the motor car was very much in its infancy. The song I recall most was 'I'm forever blowing bubbles' – everybody sang or whistled it.

The 'Late Night Extra' newsboy called out, 'Read all about it,' usually on a Sunday night. People would hear the cry, grab a penny and run into the street to find out the latest news. The last one I can remember was the death of King Albert of the Belgians in a climbing accident.

Another familiar figure eagerly watched for each evening, especially in the winter, was the lamp lighter, gradually making his way down the street.

There were many buskers playing outside the White Lion – Antonio with his accordian and, another victim of the depression, a man who played the violin beautifully; his music was so poignant and sad that it used to make me cry. He often had his crippled, motherless son with him, and my mum used to send over a glass of milk and a piece of cake for the little lad.

Joe Portch could be seen walking around with his wooden yoke on his shoulders, carrying a pail of milk on each end.

The farmers would drive in from the local farms in their horse-drawn vehicles on market day, leave them in the White Lion, and journey on to the Bristol market, which I think was on Thursdays. At lunch time the farmer's wife would come in the shop for three pennyworth of bread and cheese for her husband to eat whilst drinking his beer – no pub food in those days. Meanwhile, the wife would look around the shops or wait in the cart. Later on the drovers would arrive, driving the cattle or sheep along the High Street to or from the various farms.

Fred King or, as the locals called him, Sexton Blake, could be seen pushing his soap box on wheels, filled with his bits and pieces, around the village. His hair was cropped like a monk and he always wore a long dark brown coat down to his ankles, tied around the waist with a piece of rope. He would be called a dropout in these modern days. He was quite harmless, but the boys would tease him and then he would give chase. One time we girls were caught up in the middle and how we ran, we were breathless when we reached the shop, but it was a sort of thrill just the same.

Occasionally there was a skirmish outside the White Lion, when 'Peggy' Russell would be a combatant. He would stand on his good leg, with his back to the wall, and take on all comers. He would use his peg leg to hit the enemy in the 'tum' and they would fall like ninepins. The village Bobby would arrive and move them on and peace would return. (The spoil sport.)

Fred Palmer was the local carrier. He would carry out any commission for the locals in his horse and wagon; take parcels to the station, collect goods from any of the town shops, take pieces of furniture to a villager's relative or move them to another part of the city, collect or deliver loads of vegetables etc. I remember him taking a valuable piece of china to be riveted for my mother. Fred was a valued member of the community and was such a nice man. Sadly, he died tragically in Cooper's Barton.

Just one more early memory. Eddie Elling and I were going, with our jam pots and fishing nets, to catch minnows in the Trym – it was near a stile spanning the field and the allotments (Merlin Close area). Lena (Newman), his sister, had been despatched to fetch us home for dinner, but she decided to climb a tree and became stuck when the girdle of her gym frock caught on a branch. Eddie and I shouted advice, but all in vain, until she undid her girdle and came hurtling down, narrowly missing a dip in the Trym. We scampered home as fast as our legs could take us. Many of you will remember Lena as she stumped around the village on her stick, crippled with that wretched arthritis.

So remember, you who wait impatiently for some one to shuffle across the road, that they too once climbed trees and jumped puddles.

Mrs Betsey Symons of the Coffee Tavern and Agnes Skyrme, who became the village grocer.

Left: *Arthur Skyrme in the Cadet Corps, Merchant Venturers School, 1915.* Above: *Father at call up for the First World War when aged 47.*

The war memorial looking towards Canford Lane with the working men's institution to the left.

37

May 1914. P.C. Joby Gough on duty, watching passengers alight from tram no. 2 at the tram terminus. The Jubilee Fountain is on the right.

38

FIFTEEN

The Little Room Behind
The Shop

In spite of the years of Depression, the Great Strike and the Wall Street Crash, the business grew during the 'twenties and the little shop gradually encroached on our living room space.

The stairs were moved, so that they led directly from the shop up to what was our best upstairs room, which then doubled as a tea room, so that we only used it on Sundays, high days and holidays.

Cupboards were removed downstairs and a partition with frosted glass now separated the shop from the living room. It was a very cosy room, the thick walls making it cool in summer and warm in winter, especially when the lovely open fire was blazing away.

A large square table dominated the centre of the room, and it was here that my parents pored over the accounts, mum planned her menus, dad his garden, while my brother browsed through the sports pages or oiled his cricket bat or football boots and I struggled with my homework. I remember helping to mix the Christmas puddings on this table and of course, making a 'wish', and watching dad ice our birthday cakes.

After the shop had finally closed, supper would be served, often some of our own cooked ham or a pound of sausages or other left over 'perishable' items from the shop, because there was no refrigeration to keep these goods fresh.

Before going to bed Dad would get out the Cherry Blossom to clean and polish the family's footwear, while puffing away at his favourite pipe, and Mum busied herself putting out our clean clothes ready for the morning.

My mother often referred to the shop as the 'Half-Way House', and in our little room the country customers would be refreshed with a cup of tea – quite often they had walked in with their orders from places as far away as Lawrence Weston, Catbrain, Pilning etc. Then the farmers' wives would arrive with their eggs and butter and sort and price them on the table. The travellers would also be seen and my word, how smart most of them were with their bowler hats and rolled umbrellas, and what a joy for me if I was around when the Frys or Cadbury representative called and I could sample their wares.

In late October the rep from Budgets, the local wholesaler, would call, open up his case and take out his samples of dried fruit, all wrapped up in the traditional 'sugar bag blue' paper. Sultanas from Syria or Australia, currants from Greece or Turkey, raisins from Spain or California – each packet marked with the district where they had been grown. Such exotic names, which should we choose?

What excitement it was to see the Christmas chocolate or Easter eggs mum had chosen from the various firms' displays, held at the Bristol Hotel, when they were delivered and unpacked on the table.

Later on, when my mother had become an invalid, confined to a wheelchair, I remember her writing to Baker Bakers and they would send her a selection of dresses, hats etc. that she could choose from in her own home – what service.

In the afternoons my mother would take a little time off to have a cuppa with her cousin Florrie Rowley and Mrs Selby, her great friend from the shop across the road. It was an aggravation to me that, just as the conversation was getting interesting, I would be sent out to see if the kettle was boiling – I later suspected that this was the moment when one of the three friends imparted the latest news of who was 'expecting'.

When customers could not pay their grocery bill because of other demands, say having their husband's boots mended at Fishers or Toveys, my mother would discuss the problem with them, with the usual outcome that they arranged to pay the next week's bill on time and a shilling a week off the unpaid bill. It amazes me how my parents coped, as half the time this did not work, and yet they still paid for both my brother's and my own education, and we were always well dressed.

Yes, I can remember children being kept home from school because their only pair of shoes were being mended. Many large families were reared on a wage of not much more, and very often less, than youngsters get as pocket money today (inflation apart). The church ran clothing, boot and shoe, and coal clubs, and Miss Lennard, head of the Sunday School, presided over these on a Monday night at the village hall, when members could be seen trooping up to pay their dues.

We ran a 'Christmas Club' and each week when a customer paid her bill of say nine shillings and nine pence three farthings, the two pence farthing would be put in the back of her order book to be saved for Christmas. You can imagine the tedious job of adding up the amount at the end of the year – and we gave six pence in the pound discount!

We were often asked for old sheets for use as bandages etc. No National Health Service then, only Nurse Mizen, who was overworked, riding around on her trusty bicycle.

The Relieving Officer had a standing order for lunch whenever his duties brought him to Westbury. After his departure, the recipients of his pink (5/-) or green (10/-) slips came in for their groceries. Many a time a wife would ask, 'Could you let my old man have half an ounce of baccy' or 'a pack of Woodbines' from this money, but tobacco was a forbidden item on the list of things we were allowed to supply. This sort of request led to much sucking of pencils and crossings out until we duly presented the amended bill, hoping it looked all right, otherwise we would lose the concession if it was known we had broken the law.

I can see some of the women now, with their husbands' discarded flat caps worn back to front on their heads and a coarse apron made of sacking worn in the mornings and then a spotless white apron in the afternoons.

SIXTEEN

Mother's Pride
(No, not the bread variety)

She was rather a simple soul. Nowadays she would be classed as a one parent family, but without the benefit of Child Allowance and Social Security, and with a good deal less tolerance. I can picture her now, her round, red cheeked, placid face beaming away behind her thick pebble glasses.

One day when she came into the shop, and before she asked for her goods, she burst out, 'It's my little girl's birthday. Would you like to see her cards?'

'Oh yes, I would,' said my mum. She stretched over and gave the child a bar of Fry's Five Boys chocolate, and wished her a happy birthday. Meanwhile, her mother had dived into her capacious bag and produced a pile of cards. All the neighbours had remembered. 'Love from Mrs Brown', from 'Mrs Edwards' and 'Mr Jones', and one from the milkman, the baker and even the 'Lady at the Big House'.

'You are a lucky girl,' said Polly to the smiling couple, but as she handed the cards back, she couldn't help but notice they had one thing in common—all had the same handwriting, her mother's. Whether you call it 'Mother's Pride' or better still, 'Mother's love', this one little girl was not going to lose out.

There was also an older brother who had just started work.

'How's your boy getting on?' asked my mother. 'Oh! ever so well, he's next to the manager now,' was her reply.

'Well done,' said Polly. 'How many work there?'

'Just the two,' was the proud mother's answer.

SEVENTEEN
The Boy Cousin

A boy cousin had come to visit up at the farm. There were twenty years between him and his eldest sister, so it was understandable that he was somewhat spoilt and boisterous to boot. He had the habit of pulling flies and other insects to pieces, which revolted us three girls, but in the years to come we realised it was just a boy's curiosity to find out how things worked. He could have become a brilliant entomologist had he been given the chance. He grew up to be a big gentle fellow with a wry sense of humour. He had a great affinity with the whole of the animal world, and kept many species of birds in his garden, which he tended with loving care.

During his stay at the farm the girls' mother, who sometimes worked on a very short fuse and had had little to do with boys, became exasperated with his antics and said, 'Oh, take him down to Auntie Pob's at the shop.' They duly arrived, and he promptly started his investigation of our room behind the shop.

There are advantages and disadvantages in whatever era one happens to be born. Motor cars, radios, television, telephones, to name but a few, are all considered the norm in most homes today. In our case, to be around when these items first arrived on the scene had its compensations; for the thrill and delight we felt when owning one of these new fangled luxuries became a possibility was more than today's youngsters could possibly ever imagine.

We were one of the first to have an electric iron, and the crude fitting would make today's safety conscious shudder. There were no special power points as of now, and the iron was plugged into an ordinary light socket, which was fixed halfway up the wall, from the window seat, and left bare whenever the iron was not in use.

'What's this?' thought the boy and promptly stuck his finger in the socket. As he shot backwards across the room, he ejaculated 'Oh! Christ'. We three girls gasped and almost froze in horror. The Lord's name must never be taken in vain, we had learned at our convent school. We almost expected young Jack to disappear in a cloud of

43

smoke. On reflection, I suppose he nearly did. My mother dashed in, exclaiming, 'Whatever's going on?'

She surveyed the situation, slipped into the shop and returned with a tin of Sharp's Kreemy Toffees, saying, 'Here you are, each of you have one, and now take that boy home.'

The three silently filed out of the shop, the boy still jaunty, sucking his finger and chewing his toffee at the same time. As they reached the doorway, the older girl turned, and there was no need for words for the expression on her face said it all, 'Boys!'

EIGHTEEN

Hot Cross Buns

'Christmas comes earlier every year,' wails the harassed housewife. It doesn't, you know, but Christmas cards in August, Father Christmas in October and Easter Eggs in January only makes it seem so. It's the fault of the big stores, trying to pull a fast one on each other. The children are being bombarded by television advertising and demand gifts often way beyond the means of their parents. The children are the ones to be pitied, for they are the losers; not only have they lost out on that sense of 'awe' but on the other one, of anticipation, for it is only the very, very young – and they get younger every year – who still get the thrill of opening the Christmas stocking.

Nowadays hot cross buns are on display before the season of Lent begins, but notices used to appear in the shops only a few days before Good Friday requesting that customers order their hot cross buns. Wilkins' bakery at the top of Chock Lane supplied us with bread and cakes for our shop. (What I would give for one of their dough cakes now.) The men would work throughout the night on the eve of Good Friday, and the buns would be delivered hot first thing in the morning.

44

Not so early as Tom at the farm anticipated. He was what used to be described as 'a bit funny', but really he was, I suppose, what is now called 'a nature's child', for he had a great affinity with animals, and was noted for his skill as a drover. He knew and named every cow or sheep in his charge. He always carried a stick but never used it in anger, just to persuade the animals in which direction to go. He walked with his charges from places as far off as Thornbury or Chipping Sodbury, not far in a car, I grant you, but just imagine walking with up to fifty animals all the way to Westbury. My aunt was quite content for her young daughter to go out in the fields with him, for 'Old Tom' would not let any harm come to his little Gladdie.

One day he appeared in the shop. 'I've come for Uncle Arthur's funeral hat,' he said. The farmer was going to a funeral and had asked dad to lend him his black bowler.

'No wonder they can afford to go to the pictures every week,' sniffed my mother. 'Some people never buy if they can borrow . . .'

At this particular Easter Tom had his orders to go down early to fetch the hot cross buns. But not *that* early, for, as I was sleeping in the front above the shop, it was I who was awakened at about five o'clock, with Tom shouting, 'Aggie, Aggie, one a penny, two a penny, hot cross buns.' We let him in to await the delivery of really hot cross buns, still steaming from the oven, filled with luscious fruit and peel, at about seven o'clock.

Old Tom, with his dog Toby, was a well-known figure around the village. Came the day when he returned to the farm, tears streaming down his old rugged face, mutely holding an empty collar in his hand, for Toby had been killed crossing a road.

'Have to get another dog,' said the farmer, but Tom continued to weep, and we three girls wept with him.

Now, how did I get on to this? I was only giving to write about hot cross buns. What it is to have a grasshopper mind.

45

NINETEEN

'But That's Before My Mother Was Born!'

'It's over ten years since I left school,' I overheard a girl say as I arrived for the Annual Meeting of the Old Girls' Society. She was standing with a group of contemporaries, chatting and remembering school days.

'Well, my mother left in 1946,' said another.

As I passed I murmured, 'I left in 1926.'

Now that was a real conversation stopper. They all gasped, and one exclaimed in a voice of rising crescendo, 'But that's before my mother was born!'

No doubt she was right, for when I became a pupil at St Ursulas it was still anything but 'all quiet on the Western Front.'

Nevertheless, I well remember the day when, with my two young cousins, and accompanied by a much older cousin, we trotted up from Westbury village to the Convent. We had been summoned to attend an interview in order to be assessed as suitable material for the school.

The bell was pulled . . . we waited expectantly . . . a face appeared at the grille, our mission was stated, the door opened, and we were ushered along the cloister and shown into a little room. Our hearts were beating a little faster, for we were in a state of awe, a condition I suspect not often experienced by the young of today. I think that maybe they miss out somewhat, for I have found that a little awe, mystery, wonderment or whichever way you describe it, just adds something more to the spice of life.

However, we must have passed muster, for young Dorothy and I were accepted. The actual interview has become a little hazy and the only question our older cousin – now in her 95th year – laughingly remembers being asked was, 'Do the children usually wear gloves?' She, quick thinking, replied, 'Oh yes, we left them outside in the pram.'

With the beginning of the new term, our lives moved on into the next phase, for we had become pupils of St Ursula's High School.

Our last inspection was to descend the stone steps leading to the two cellars, all dark and creepy – lovely.

Both girls celebrated their 21st birthdays at East Hill, then it was sold for the building of Cote Lea Park and Pinewood Close. I wonder whose house or garden stands above the site of the cellars, for they must have been filled with rubble. Of the events celebrated at the farm, the most memorable was Big Doll's wedding.

TWENTY TWO
The Wedding Of The Year
July 3rd 1922

You couldn't be more wrong if you thought 'Wedding Of The Year' meant one of those grand affairs which keep you glued to the television for hours on end. No, ours was when our 'special friend' told us she was going to be married.

She is now in her 98th year, a little bent and not very steady on her pins, but with a mind still sharp as a razor's edge. Many of you will know her as Dorothy Sims, but to us she was 'Big Doll'. It was more than a minor irritation to her mother when her youngest brother, Harry Rowley, named his first born Dorothy, and the two cousins became known as Big Doll and Little Doll.

Although she was quite a bit older than Little Doll, Gladys (her younger sister) and I, we three never thought of Big Doll as a 'Grown-Up' and she acted as a buffer between us and our elders.

It was to her that we went to seek consolation when we imagined we were hard done by and it was she who played the piano when we gave our Sunday evening impromptu concerts with our long suffering parents as a captive audience.

She helped with all the activities connected with Mena House Farm, the sheep shearing and the hay making – we thought she looked like Queen Boadicea in her chariot as she drove the horse and rake around the fields where the houses of Ridgeway and surrounding roads now stand.

Sometimes she would take the three of us with her on her journeys down to the village and back to the farm, laughingly threatening to throw the pig-net over us if we did not keep still in the back of the cart. Great times and now perhaps you can understand why we thought of her as our 'special friend' and now she was going to be married – and with what joyful anticipation we looked forward to this event.

A week or so before the wedding the two Dorothy's, Dad and I walked from our shop up to Charlton Common where Uncle Charlie and his family lived at Chestnut Farm to deliver the wedding invitation.

We jumped over the stile where Shipley Road now starts, past the back of Dudden's Farm, (now Whytes Close) with its ever pervading smell of celery and pigs, hardly stepping on a road surface until we reached our destination.

It was a beautiful summer's evening and Little Doll and I were hot and thirsty when we arrived and were very grateful when offered a long cool drink. We downed the lot without pausing for breath and then Auntie Annie said to her boys, Jim and Jack, 'take the girls and show them your collection of birds eggs.'

As we walked down the wide whitewashed passage the walls seemed to cave in and the eggs seemed to be over-flowing out of their boxes. 'I feel ever so funny,' said Little Doll. 'So do I,' I replied with a giggle. What we did not know was that we had been given a glass of Farm House cider which was made in a port wine barrel.

It was years before it dawned on us that it was our first experience of being tipsy!

As the wedding day drew near, the village became a hive of industry. My mother was up to her elbows cooking for the occasion while a splendid wedding cake was on display in Sims the bakers shop window, for the bridegroom to be was Morley, the older son of Mr and Mrs Frank Sims and every day little knots of people could be seen looking in the window admiring the masterpiece.

The wedding breakfast and reception was to be held at East Hill Farm, the home of the bride's aunt and uncle, Mr and Mrs Harry

July 1922. Wedding of the Year, between Dorothy Rowley and Morley Sims. Taken on the lawn at East Hill Farm, now Cole Lea Park and Pinewood Close.

Rowley.

At this time it was the custom to lend items such as the cutlery, plates, cups and saucers to cater for the influx of relations and friends on such an occasion. Each piece had its own coloured piece of cotton carefully attached to denote whose house it had come from.

On the morning of the wedding, my mum was up at the crack of dawn making jellies, blancmange and trifles. Stacks of sandwiches were cut, the hams having already been cooked in readiness.

Up at the farm, strawberries and raspberries were freshly picked, the butter and cream having been made the day before.

Over at the bakery, the men did not need any urging to make a special effort with their delicious cakes and fancies and, all in good time, everything was delivered up to East Hill Farm.

Strange to say, I cannot remember the actual wedding ceremony but I do remember the feastings, especially the strawberries and cream!

Morley was supported by his brother, Jack, who was best man. Mabel, the bride's sister, who later was to marry my brother Arthur, was bridesmaid.

Eventually we all assembled on the lawn for the official photographs to be taken and, just like all royal children, the children of nearly seven decades ago sat on the ground in the front row. And who was plonked right in the middle? Yes – you've guessed it, Little Doll, young Gladdie and me.

East Hill Farm, its fields and gardens, are now lost for ever under the concrete of Cote Lea Park and Pinewood Close, but I should like to imagine that on a summer's evening mingling with the breeze, could still be heard an echo of laughter from that happy day so many years ago. For really and truly it certainly was a great village occasion.

THE FORTIES
A MOST
MOMENTOUS
DECADE

Part Two
The Forties – A Most Momentous Decade

The Forties	57
The Years Between	59
'The Things Are Up'	62
They Also Served Who Stood And Weighed	64
'And A Box Of Crystallized Fruits Please'	72
Stand Up My Girl, We're English	74
Let's Go To The Pictures	75
And All Because . . .	76
The Dancing Years	78
Anyone Seen My Petrol Coupons?	79
Thanksgiving At St. Paul's	81
Freedom, But At What A Cost!	82
The Victory Parade	83
The End Of A Momentous Decade	85

ONE

The Forties

And I said to the man that stood at the gate of the year
Give me a light that I may tread safely into the unknown
And he replied
'Go out into the darkness
'And put your hand into the hand of God,
'That shall be to you better than light,
'And safer than a known way.'

This was the Christmas message of King George VI to his people, who were now standing with their backs to the wall.

As I let my mind roam through the years of this decade, it is as if holding a kaleidoscope, and with every shake a different picture appears . . . of war, ration books, sirens, gun-fire, blackouts, queues, coupons, shortages, restrictions . . . but above all the camaraderie.

As I delved deeper, I realised it was a much more traumatic, very poignant time, for, early in 1940, my mother was released from the bondage of her crippled body, the pain of which had become more excruciating over the past eighteen years. She was a most courageous lady if ever there was one, with a great sense of humour, very, very strict, firm but fair. Her chief desire was to see her children receive a better education than she had had.

She never hesitated to 'call a spade a spade', which sometimes made me wince, but was nevertheless at everyone's beck and call, whether from family, friend, customer or stranger.

I once read of a son, who asked his mother, 'Why are you so cross?', and her reply was, 'Because I care.' In other words, 'because I love you.' So it was with my mum.

So once again it was all change in the village, as one by one, familiar faces disappeared, as they went off to serve King and Country – Bill Holliday and his brother-in-law, Frank Mumford, Ernie Lippiate, Wally Long, and our newsagent neighbour, Bill Smith, to name but a

57

few, leaving the old men and women to 'keep the home fires burning.'

LEST WE FORGET

My cousin Gladys was now engaged to her Jack, and they had spent a happy, carefree evening together. Within an hour or so of their parting he lay dead. A lone plane, returning from a raid on Manchester, dropped its last bomb and scored a direct hit on the camp on Bedminster Down.

Their Uncle Charles, who lived only a mile away, at Chestnut Farm in Charlton Common, his wife, Ann, and elder son Jim, were killed by a bomb blast as they sat in their air raid shelter. Ironically, the farmhouse stood intact, the supper laid ready for their return.

A family of three generations, this time on their mother's side, lay dead under the rubble of their home in Falmouth.

Lena (Elling) Newman rang.

'Could you get Eddie. I think the phone's out of order. I would like a word with him.' I ran across the road to fetch him. He came and took the call and left shaking his head, visibly moved.

'It is as I feared,' he murmured. His sister had just been informed that her husband, Percy, had been reported missing.

The evening before was the first one thousand bomber raid on Germany.

Dorothy (Howard's) fun loving sister Gwen, early in 1941 married her Scottish soldier sweetheart, but within the month she too lay dead, again without warning, this time by a deadly virus.

There was no blood strain between me and any of those good folk, nevertheless, they were all part of my extended family, and I mourned for them.

TWO

The Years Between

Westbury is really two villages, more so in my growing up days. Westbury Court Farm, the Police Station and the Hole in the Wall virtually divided the shopping area. The top part expanded after the selling of Westbury Court Farm – shops were built in Canford Lane, as was the Carlton Cinema, with more shops at the top of the High Street. On the opposite side of the High Street, the Co-op came and another three or four shops.

But for us, at the bottom of the village, from the 'White Horse' to the 'White Lion', there was hardly a ripple of change.

Horses were still being shod in the High Street. You could buy bread freshly baked on the premises at Sims or Longs. Cream was made daily at George's Dairy. You could watch your shoes being repaired at Fisher's or Tovey's, and, up at The Rosery tea could be taken in the pleasant gardens which were dotted around with little summer houses. Customers for flowers or vegetables were content to wait while Mr or Mrs Preston, the parents of David and John, popped out and cut the produce fresh from the garden, as they could while away the waiting time studying the fascinating maps of old Bristol which adorned the walls of the little shop.

The Rev. H.J. Wilkins, who was the Vicar of Westbury for over forty years, was still at the Church, ably supported by the well known Westbury family, the Underdowns, who were part and parcel of the life of the Church and Village Hall.

The only changes were the building of the New Post Office on the site of Cooper's Barton, Price's, the corn chandler, became The Westbury Motor and Carriage Works and petrol pumps now appeared in the village, while the first Westbury Labour Exchange at 48 High Street opened its doors.

The shopkeepers' children grew up, left school, and many joined their parents in the business, but inevitably, the years have taken their toll, and now only one of the old family names remain, Mogfords. They were the first to have the telephone, with Westbury 1 as their

59

number. The Westbury exchange was in Westbury Hill. Long live 'Moggies'.

In case this sounds all too idyllic, we all had our ups and downs. Our particular bugbear was the flipping Trym – far too often we became Westury-*in*-Trym, for, with monotonous regularity, the river burst its banks and poured through our shop and living quarters. Our beautiful parquet shop floor, which I have mentioned previously, gradually rotted away and had to be replaced with cement—Ugh!

The winds of change were already in the air, and the crux was reached on September 3rd 1939.

Most of the shopkeepers were classified as Reserved Occupations, especially the ones in the food trades, nevertheless, many familiar faces disappeared from the village. The able-bodied men either joined the Home Guard or became A.R.P. Wardens, while we lesser mortals became Street Wardens, or were we called Fire Watchers?

One evening we assembled in the old dairy and stable yard just off Henbury Road for our first practice. Jimmy Greig, the blacksmith, was our C. in C., supported by Bill Smith. We stood around with our stirrup pumps and buckets of water. Jimmy said, 'When I say "Water on" begin to pump.'

Now if Dorothy had been paying attention instead of chatting to Evelyn Tovey, the shoemaker's wife, and Mrs Anstee, the fish and chip lady, she would have heard the command, 'Water on' – furthermore, she would have noticed how she was holding the hose. As it was, our two instructors received the full force of water on their persons, it even put out Jimmy's pipe! The whole company, including the two victims, collapsed with laughter and the meeting broke up, somewhat in confusion. As we giggled our way back to our shops and homes my father was heard to murmur, 'If we have you lot to depend on, heaven help us.'

Now we really had our backs to the wall, as Hitler's armies rampaged through Europe. All the gates and railings of the shops and houses were taken away to be melted down for firearms. Dorothy and I came back with van loads of pots and pans, collected from our customers, for these too were melted down for the same purpose.

We sold Savings Certificates, helped with the salvage collections, as well as coping with rations, which became smaller and smaller. Road signs were removed, directories taken out of the telephone boxes and delivery vans had their names and addresses painted over. The word invasion was never far from our minds.

I have many memories of our fire watching days, but one will suffice. It was a very cold, dark night, the siren had sounded and search lights were sweeping the skies. We were all very warmly clad and standing around outside our shops when suddenly the whole village was as light as day, as flares began to gently drop down. Then a stick of incendiaries clattered down. The fire bombs dropped all along the High Street; luckily the majority fell either in the road or on the pavement. I saw my father, with his First World War tin hat on and smoking his pipe upside down (in case the enemy spotted the glow!) and Mr Selby, the barber, both men in their seventies, dashing around dropping sandbags on the bombs. Meanwhile, Mr Pratt came out of his garage and said, 'Agnes, lend me a hand, I've got one between three cars.' He carried the water, I followed with the pump and, with Mrs Pratt and Barbara, we worked our way down the darkened garage until we found our bomb. 'Pump Agnes,' said Mr P. – our instructions were to first let a gentle spray play on the bomb, but in my enthusiasm I pumped too vigorously and the nozzle flew off the end and a brilliant white light lit up the whole place and was it hot! However, we soon got it under control and were not harmed.

The guns on the Henbury Golf Links blazed away and we heard later that the Officer in Charge had said, 'Look at the little village in the valley – get help to them quickly or they will be wiped out,' but he was astonished at how quickly darkness fell in the streets again – Jimmy and Bill had taught us well.

THREE

'The Things Are Up'

She was a rather posh customer; she looked so elegant in her summer silk suit, her large brimmed hat, long gloves and high heeled shoes. She had popped her head around the shop door to ask, 'I don't suppose you have a bar of chocolate?' I bent down under the counter, where such goodies were kept for 'registered customers only'.

As she waited, she remarked, 'The things are up,' the things being the barrage balloons which ringed the city at various times during the Second World War. I am afraid that we had become rather blasé about such matters. It was the time of the so called Phoney War. We were so safe, they said, several lines of defence between us and the French coast, they said. Bristol was safe, let alone our village.

Then the siren, sometimes referred to as the 'Si-reen', situated on top of the Police Station in the High Street, began to wail. It was a glorious sunny day, with a bright blue sky, the sound of planes approaching could be heard. All up and down the High Street shopkeepers and their customers, including Dorothy and our posh customer, were in their doorways, gazing upwards. Meanwhile, I had found a Mars bar, or was it a Fry's Turkish Delight?

'Come on out, it's a lovely sight,' they cried. The aeroplanes looked like silver dragonflies in the sky as they flew in formation. Yes, it was a lovely sight, but Bill Smith, the newsagent next door, was shouting, 'For God's sake get back – they're Jerries.' Bill was an A.R.P. Warden and later joined the R.A.F.

The gunfire was heard and everyone disappeared. The High Street became as empty as a Victorian Sabbath day, except for one old lady, who was toddling down for her midday tipple. As she reached The White Lion the door slammed in her face. 'Let me in, let me in,' she cried, as she banged on the door. The door half opened, an arm shot out and she was pulled in.

Bombs could now be heard screaming down. At first I thought it was our neighbour, Mrs Anstee, having hysterics! The three of us dived under the table, shredded wheat and such like raining down on us. It seemed like eternity, but it was only a minute or so before the 'All Clear' sounded.

We crawled out, our customer's hat slightly askew. The blacksmith went back to his smithy, the butcher's boy carried on loading his van, Dorothy and I resumed weighing up the weekly rations, and Blackie, our cat, strolled out from behind a pile of empty cardboard boxes, tail held high, and in the nonchalent feline way, resumed sunning himself on top of the biscuit tins.

For a brief moment our village had been caught up in 'Hitler's War' but, just as suddenly, normality returned, and after a rueful survey of the broken shop windows, it was a case of business as usual.

AFTERMATH – Houses were damaged in Falcondale Road, Henleaze and Southmead, including a direct hit on The Larches in Eastfield. But the real target was The Drome at Filton, which suffered a grievous loss of life and extensive damage.

FOUR

They Also Served Who Stood And Weighed

Winston Churchill's voice, thundering over the radio, was a source of inspiration, hope and pride in our nation.

In one of his speeches he uttered the words, 'They also serve who stand and wait.' He was referring to the people on the home front, especially when invasion threatened, those watching on the coast, those manning the gun-sites and the balloon barrages, the A.R.P. and the fire watchers.

We on the food front SERVED, STOOD AND WEIGHED not in glamorous looking uniforms, but in overalls, which, in spite of our being allowed extra clothing coupons, got shabbier by the year. There was also the problem of the soap ration.

Seven o'clock in the morning and it was out in the shop, weighing up the rations, which varied according to the stocks and replacements held in the country. Oh dear, we did seem to have more families of three registered with us, 'the awkward lot'. Families of four were a doddle, but for threes it was 12 oz sugar, 9 oz butter, 6 oz margarine, 3 oz lard and $4\frac{1}{2}$ oz cheese.

It was truly amazing how many families suddenly had a vegetarian in the family. Up to now, vegetarians were thought cranks. By sacrificing one meat ration, you could have 12 oz cheese. Heavy workers were also allowed a bigger portion of cheese.

There was no such thing as an eight hour day; you worked on and on, not until you finished, for you never finished. There were coupons to count, forms to fill in, goods packed away and shelves to fill. No, you never finished, just stopped, to replenish the 'inner man' and have a breather. We gave thanks when the siren on the Police Station roof remained silent, but if they wailed, on went the fire watching tin helmets, shaped like an upturned chamber pot, which didn't do much for our morale. Our friend from across the road, Olive Swayne, an A.R.P. warden, looked quite glamorous as she stopped for a chat, her helmet tilted at an angle, or wearing her heavy government-issued navy blue coat.

As we stood outside our homes and shops in the black-out, the tediousness was relieved by chats with passers-by. One man in particular was a regular member of our group; he was just a voice in the dark, but when normality returned, he made his identity known.

'Oh!' I exclaimed, 'You are Mr Stone.' (Actually he only lived just around the corner at Trym House.)

'Yes, I am,' he said, held out his hand and said, 'How do you do Miss Skyrme,' and I replied, 'How do you do Mr Stone.'

'It doesn't look as though it's going to be us tonight,' said a voice, as planes roared overhead and away up country, probably to Birmingham, Manchester, or other towns and cities. We gave a sigh of relief for this night's reprieve, and a silent prayer for those others who were going to 'cop it'.

Apart from 'the common round, the daily task', we sold savings certificates, were in charge of the waste paper collection, and used our half-day off to deliver the country orders. Well, it made a change from being behind the counter.

A decree went out for householders to donate any old pots and pans to be melted down to help the war effort, and we came home from one of our trips with a van load of these utensils. People stood at their doors waving an old kettle or saucepan.

Dorothy would nip smartly out of the van, run up the path, and a beaming lady would hand over her 'mite'.

'Good many breakfasts been cooked in that old pan,' she said, 'but as long as it helps.' This was said, almost wistfully, as she watched it join the other pile in the back of the van. We cheerfully sang, 'There'll always be an England,' or 'Run, rabbit, run,' as we rattled our way back to the shop.

Then there were the times we had to placate our customers.

'My sister got a jelly at Drew's. Why?'

'Mumfords had back bacon this week. Why?'

'This is the third week without an egg ration. Why?'

'Up at the Co-op . . .' They!! They!! They!!

Hopefully, the ball would sometimes be in our court.

My father, usually the most courteous of men, came back exasperated. 'Old Mother so-and-so didn't half create, because she didn't have a box of matches. Said she didn't have one last week. "Can't send what we haven't got," I said.'

'Never mind Dad,' said Dorothy. 'Sit down, and I'll make a cup of tea.'

To say the last morning of the rationing period was hectic would be an understatement, for every coupon and point had to be used up or else lost for ever. I remember one such Saturday morning, and at five minutes to one o'clock Dorothy, who had household duties, as well as those in the shop, glanced up and muttered,

'Just look at them, still pouring in, and I haven't put the spuds on yet.'

A customer stood gazing at the one lone coupon left in her book.

'What shall I have?' she pondered.

'Come on, come on,' I thought.

'I know,' she said brightly. 'I'll have a quarter of a pound of rice.'

'Oh Lord, give me a bag, where's the scoop?'

'There you are then. Two pence please.'

No wonder as the Open sign was turned to Closed I said,

'Let's have a breather. I'm tired of being nice.'

But the peace was rudely shattered, as a hissing sound came from the kitchen.

'Oh, gosh,' said Dorothy, hastily jumping up. 'The spuds are boiling over.'

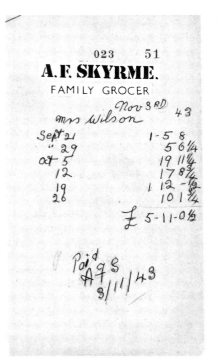

How's that for a six weeks' grocery account?
But it was 50 years ago.

This is a true example of a weekly grocery
order for a family of three 50 years ago
(including delivery to the door).

The proprietor outside his shop, now The Villager.

My parents and Doris showing off the new delivery bike outside our shop in 1920.

Above: *Playmates Dorothy and Gladys Rowley.* Left: *Dorothy and Gladys, all 'Growed Up'.*

Harvest Festival at Westbury Church in 1934.

71

FIVE

'And A Box Of Crystallized Fruits Please'

'Good heavens,' I exclaimed to Dorothy. 'Just look at the price of those crystallized fruits; £3.95 for a small box'. She grinned.

'Are you remembering what I'm remembering?' I certainly was, for although over forty years had passed, it seemed like only yesterday.

She was a rather tiny lady, but what she lacked in height she made up for in other ways, quite perky really. Always smart, and never without gloves. With the approach of winter months out came her fur coat, and then we knew what to expect. She would perch herself on the chair at the counter and proceed to give her order, and, with a wicked look in her eye, always concluded, 'and a box of crystallized fruits please,' knowing darn well that not for love nor money, or even sweet coupons, were we going to see these goodies for many a long year to come.

Having finished, she would rise to her full four feet eleven, and, wrapping her fur coat firmly around herself, would sail towards the door, but not before someone rushed to open it for her, and, with a somewhat sickly grin, wish her good day and thank you; and she, still with that wicked gleam, would reply, 'Good day to you too.'

Christmases came and Christmases went, but the day came when things became a little easier. Each time orders arrived from the wholesalers it was like opening our stockings on Christmas morning – we never knew what we might find. Lo and behold, one week we found three boxes of crystallized fruits. We just couldn't wait for Thursday morning to come.

'I'm serving her,' I said, but I wondered why the girls were in no hurry for their elevenses, and hovered around.

She duly arrived to give her order, the fur coat now beginning to look a little mangy, and as usual the final item was 'and a box of crystallized fruits please.'

'Certainly', I said, and dived under the counter and produced the longed for item. 'Ten shillings and sixpence; shall we send it or will you take it?' At last the shoe was on the other foot. She seemed to shrink within her old fur coat as she whispered 'Thank you.'

She never really wanted a box of crystallized fruits, just enjoyed teasing us over the years.

As usual, someone rushed to open the door, and several pairs of eyes twinkled as the owners chorused out 'Good morning.' Mrs M, the old lady, turned, and with a quirky smile, called back, 'Good morning girls.'

'I'd better put the kettle on,' said Dorothy, and the girls sat around in the room behind the shop, having their rather late elevenses. I could hear them having a giggle as they talked over our hour of triumph. Yes, it was a good moment.

SIX

Stand Up My Girl, We're English

When invasion appeared imminent we, the food retailers, were issued with three months' supplies of rationed goods according to the number of customers we had registered with us, but at the end of each four weeks we had to account for every ounce of butter and every jar of jam or marmalade. It was called 'sending in the returns', or some such thing, but it seems a long time ago now. On the form we had to state what we started with, what we sold, and how much we had left. It was a task I loathed, and if it tallied, it was more than a miracle.

On this particular night, I was on my hands and knees, with my head stuck under the stairs, trying to count the jars of jam and marmalades.

THE SIREN SOUNDED

Mrs Dorothy Smith, our newsagent and neighbour, and my father were already outside on fire watch duty.

An A.R.P. warden shouted in the shop, 'Come out at once.'

There was heavy gunfire overhead and shrapnel was dapping down in the road. The over-excited warden ordered us to get down and crawl up the road. We had only crawled a few yards, when my father said, 'Get up my girl, we're English, and if we are going to cop it, it will be standing on our feet, not crawling on our stomachs'.

Meanwhile, Dorothy Smith, who thought she was following my dad, exclaimed, 'Oh, isn't it awful Mr Skyrme?'

Later on, when the All Clear sounded, she laughingly told us the reply she got was, 'I ain't Mr Skyrme, but you can hang on if you like missus.'

He had probably come out of the White Lion and got caught up in the affray.

SEVEN

Let's Go To The Pictures

'Oh, blow it,' I said to Dorothy. 'Let's drop everything and go to the pictures.'

For an hour or so we were wafted away to another world, another time. We drooled over the young handsome Michael Redgrave. Dorothy gave me a poke.

'What about Dad down there on his own,' she said.

I was abruptly brought back to reality, for my ever alert friend had noticed the message superimposed over the screen.

'Heavy gunfire overhead. Please do not use your torch when leaving the cinema.'

I had been too wrapped up watching the hero winning his lady.

We crept out, almost tumbled down the steps of the Orpheus and ran along Fallodon Way, keeping close to the fences, as shrapnel was dapping down on pavement and road. We popped into the shelter on the edge of the Downs for a breather. When the sounds of planes and gunfire faded, we continued our journey, and were thankful to see the sturdy figure of my father standing outside the shop, smoking his pipe upside down, in case the enemy spotted the glow, and wearing his First World War tin hat.

'Where've 'ee bin?' he reproached us, thinking we had only gone to our own Carlton Cinema, for, like all caring parents, he was so relieved to see us, he could have given us a jolly good slap. 'Well, get cracking,' he continued, 'we've all been ordered to go to the shelters. They reckon it's going to be a rough night.'

Our shelter was over behind Drew's Store, on the site of what was once Fishponds Cottages.

Next day we all had our tale to tell. We related how we had run into the Downs' shelter.

'Lot of good that would have done,' said a voice from the back of the shop. 'He haven't got no top on.'

Oh, well, you know the old saying, 'Where ignorance is bliss'.

75

EIGHT

And All Because Not One, But Two, Ladies Loved Milk Tray

'Tell us a story,' the young ones said, 'a story about when you and Grandma were young.' It was half-term, and my god-daughter's children had come on a visit.

'No! A fairy story,' the littlest one cried. 'I like fairy stories.'

So this was the result, a combination of truth and fancy.

———————

It was Saturday morning, and I still remained in the cardboard box which had housed all six of us boxes of Milk Tray. Not only was it Saturday morning, but the last of the rationing month, when all the sweet coupons had to be used up, or lost for ever. I was getting desperate. I was so lonely, and I did so want to go to a lovely family.

Whilst in my dark box, I heard of one box going to a lady who had saved her coupons to buy a treat for her grandchild. Another, a mother, had given her coupons to help her soldier son on leave buy Milk Tray for his girlfriend, yet another box being posted to a little boy who had been evacuated to the country.

I heard the Church clock strike twelve. Oh dear, only another hour to go to closing time. At this moment there was a lull in the shop, and Betty, the shopgirl, came to tidy up the shelf.

'Oh, look,' she cried, 'here's another box of Milk Tray.' She took me out, dusted me down, wrote a ticket which said, 'Only eight coupons.' I was that excited.

The time ticked on, and suddenly the shop was filled with the usual last minute rush of customers. I saw a gentle little lady peer in her ration book and say, 'I'll have that box of Milk Tray please. I've just enough coupons left.'

'Oh no you won't,' came a shrill voice from the back of the shop.

'It's mine and I am going to have it. I saw it first.'

Quite a scuffle occurred. Poor Betty didn't know what to do. The little lady fluttered and nearly gave in. 'Now, now,' said the big man. 'Fair's fair. This lady was first, don't you all agree?'

'Yes, yes,' chorused the rest of the customers.

The stranger stalked out through the door, muttering, 'I'll never go in that shop again.'

'Oh, well,' said the shopkeeper. 'She wasn't a regular anyway.'

Later that evening, with the black-out safely fastened to the windows, my little lady and her hubby sat by the fireside, listening to Tommy Handley on the wireless, chuckling away and enjoying the contents of the box.

'I'll keep this box for ever,' she said. 'It's such a lovely colour.'

'Yes,' said her hubby. 'It's the same colour as the dress you wore when we first met.'

I felt so good, and I heard a voice, not from the past, but from a long way in the future, saying with a chuckle:

'And all because not only one, but two, ladies loved Milk Tray.'

This story is based on a true incident in our shop. The second customer had noticed the chocolates when she was in the shop earlier on, and had popped home for her ration book. Hence the outburst.

NINE
The Dancing Years

At times the daily round, the common task, became more than irksome, so the chance to do something different was seized upon with alacrity. There seemed to be a lull with the air raids; even London was quiet.

'So what about it?' said Val. 'Fancy a trip up to London town to see Ivor Novello (yes, he himself) in his musical, "The Dancing Years"'. How she got the tickets or whether we took a chance is too long ago to remember, but what was so remarkable was that I was given permission to take my young niece, Pat. What an enchanting evening, even though my mind was full of catching the train back to Bristol and we left before the end of the performance.

We pushed our way along the row, murmuring, 'Sorry, sorry!' and emerged into the black-out by a different door from that which we had entered. Powerful searchlights swept the sky and we were proper flummoxed.

'Please, please,' we asked every stranger in town, and got the same reply in a variety of languages or accents, from 'Non, non,' to 'Sorry luv.'

With five minutes to spare, we reached Paddington, dragging along young Pat. We rushed up the steps and weaved between the uniformed crowds which had disgorged from a troop train. We reached the platform, only to see our train slowly, even majestically, puffing its way off to Bristol.

Hours later, we arrived at Temple Meads, no taxis around, and ran to the phone box, no reply. We started the long trek home. I rang from every phone box we passed – at Baldwin Street, the Centre, Park Street, Queens Road, and it was at Whiteladies Road that I got a reply. My brother's agitated voice said, 'Stay where you are. I'll bring the car,' a risk in itself, as private cars were banned at the time. He went to the shop and aroused dad. 'Get in,' he barked on his arrival. 'Your mother's frantic,' he said to his one and only little ewe lamb. Val sized up the situation and beat a hasty retreat, saying,

'I've only got a road or two to go.'

In deadly silence, we arrived home, without further incident, and as for me, I was in the dog house for weeks.

TEN

Anyone Seen My Petrol Coupons?

Calamity, calamity, has anyone seen my petrol coupons?

Talk about panic stations, we even looked in the fridge and gas oven and other ridiculous places, but all to no avail. Nothing else for it but to go and ring the Ministry of something or other.

'Sorry,' they said, 'you must first go and swear before a Commissioner of Oaths.' *Swear*!! I was already on the verge of that.

What now? There was no 'Law man' practising in the village. Every customer heard of my predicament and all tried to be helpful.

'I know of a chap down in Park Street,' said one. 'Shall I make an appointment for you?'

'Yes please,' I said, so I duly presented myself, inwardly trembling, outwardly endeavouring to keep an 'Englishman's stiff upper lip' like my dad taught me.

'Now,' said the stern looking man, facing me across the large leather topped desk, 'what do you think happened to your petrol coupons?' My mouth got drier and drier, then I remembered a quip of my father's, 'It's a fool that has no excuse and a rogue that has one.'

I had about 10 seconds to decide whether to be classed a fool or a rogue and decided on the latter.

'Well,' I stuttered, 'we had a flood the other day and the river Trym ran through our premises. A lot of things were swept away, so I think perhaps, er, er, er,' (What a load of old codswallop!).

79

Did I detect suspicion of a smile on the 'Law man's' face?

'Very well then,' he said. 'Stand up, put your left hand on the bible, raise your right one and say after me, "I swear by Almighty God," ' etc. etc., that I'm not trying to cadge some extra petrol or words to that effect.

'Now off you go, and I will see that you get your coupons as soon as possible.' I was so grateful I nearly curtsyed and walked out backwards.

The years rolled on until one day I opened a book and exclaimed, 'Look what I've found. It's me petrol coupons.'

'Better late than never,' said Dorothy.

I didn't throw them away. I put them away with my other memorabilia. Come 1957 and the Suez affair, and petrol coupons were issued again, in the same pink colour.

My impish sense of humour (of which a customer accused me) surfaced. I stuck my old coupons in the breast pocket of my overall, with the tops just showing.

'That's not petrol coupons?' queried a customer.

'Yes tis,' said she. 'Like one?'

'Oh thanks.' Now it was his turn to almost walk out backwards.

A FEW DAYS LATER

'I could knock your block off,' said he. However, he remained a customer. After all, they were petrol coupons. I only forgot to mention they were issued during the Second World War.

As the rationing years progressed, a red dye was added to petrol for commercial vehicles (like my old van) to avoid it being used in a private car, for a sneaky trip down to Severn Beach maybe.

ELEVEN

Thanksgiving At St. Paul's

The actual date escapes me, but my cousin Dorothy and I, plus two kids (I've always seemed to have a youngster or two in tow), were going up to the capital.

The war in Europe had ended and a Service of Thanksgiving was being held at St. Paul's. Dorothy, with her superb sense of direction, got us within hailing distance of the Cathedral. It was a beautiful sunny day and, with a measure of great excitement, we joined the hordes of people lining the streets. As the distant cheers became closer, she held me up in her arms, so that I could film the coaches as they passed.

In the first one rode their Majesties, King George VI, his consort, now the beloved Queen Mum, and their two young daughters. They were followed by the exiled Royals, Chiefs of the Armed Forces and other notables. When the roar of the crowds rose to a crescendo, Dorothy promptly dropped me, for it was the nation's hero, Churchill, who came by, so we cheered and waved with the rest. At this moment of triumph, who would have thought that before the end of the war in the east he would be rejected.

On the return journey to Bristol I lay back with my eyes closed. The two girls prattled happily away, listing all the famous people they had seen. 'It was King Kong, wasn't it?' said one to the other. 'No, my dear,' I murmured, 'it was King Haakon VII of Norway.'

TWELVE

Freedom, But At What A Cost!

We jumped at it, yes really jumped at it.

How marvellous, we said, for we had been offered some soap powder off the ration, and all above board.

It's called 'Freedom' said the elderly rep, and sells at sixpence a pound (2½p nowadays), but you will have to weigh it up as it comes in a half hundredweight bag. That's O.K. we replied.

The customers were delighted when we told them the good news, and they promised to bring their own paper bags, for paper was still short and bags were used over and over again.

Mrs Luce, a lady with the stature of an opera singer and a voice to go with it, offered her services with the weighing up. This chore was always done in the evening – just as well there was no television to watch.

Our little group of three assembled, scoops at the ready. Mrs Luce elected to fill the bags, Dorothy to weigh, and me to pack. As I ripped open the top a cloud of acrid dust rose up.

'Phew!' gasped Mrs Luce, as she manfully tried to fill the bags.

'Gosh,' said I, 'my throat is nearly raw.'

'I'll get some silk scarves to wrap round our mouths,' said the ever helpful Dorothy. Thus protected, we completed our task, but were our public grateful? Not on your life.

'Just look at my hands,' said one (no rubber gloves in those days). They were all red and sore.

'It's ruined my undies,' wailed another, 'and they were a gift from an American friend.'

'You can keep your Freedom' was the general verdict.

Oh well, we did try!

As for our friend, Mrs Luce, it was soon plain to see (or rather to hear) that she would never become a Dame Kiri Te Kanawa, for 'Freedom' had put paid to that (and it was only sixpence a pound).

THIRTEEN

The Victory Parade

When the laughter subsided, and having wiped the tears from their eyes, they said, 'How we envy you having lived through the war.'

Our eyebrows shot up – 'Envy?' we gasped, as we recalled those lost years, the air raids, the black-out, the rationing, the 'make do and mend', the kitchen front and 'dig for victory'. Above all, we remembered those friends, and all the others, who had lost or given their lives, either in war or an air raid.

'What on earth do you mean?' we queried. 'Well, you seemed to have such a togetherness, which, in spite of our so called affluent society, we seem to lack.'

Once again the god-daughters, with their young, had come to visit, and it was the usual case of, 'Tell us a story, a story about when you and Grandma were young.'

With a grin, Val turned to me and said, 'Remember the pullover I knitted for Neville?'

Now you could be excused if you thought that two girls, Convent educated, particularly back in the 'twenties, would have at least turned out to be good needlewomen. Not so. To this day I mentally give myself a pat on the back when the button I have sewn on is in line with the hole.

Either we didn't have the aptitude, or we whiled away the time dreaming, as we sat behind the counter and 'minded' the shop in the evenings, so that our Mums could have a breather.

Oh no, you kids, it wasn't all milk and honey, or rather candy and choc, just because your mother had a sweet shop.

'I think I shall knit a pullover for Neville,' said Val. 'It will keep him warm when he is on duty. I think I can spare a few coupons for the wool.'

Neville was an architect, and in a Reserved Occupation, but he was also a Captain of the Home Guard. Civilians worked by day in their jobs, and evenings and weekends were spent on duty as members of the Home Guard, A.R.P., and the humblest of us as Fire Watchers, guarding our homes and shops.

_____

It was at the time of the so-called Phoney War when Val started on the pullover.

'How's it going?' I asked. 'Well, I've made a start,' was the reply. 'I've cast on the stitches.'

Then Hitler started on the ravage of Europe – Belgium capitulated, Paris fell, Denmark and Norway were occupied. The tragedy, yet miracle, of Dunkirk, and all this time Val furiously knitted away, and each time the answer to my query was, 'A bit slow, but coming on.'

Pearl Harbour, and America entered the war, Montgomery and Rommel, locked in combat in the desert. The slog continued, both on the war and civilian front, and each time, 'A bit slow, but coming on.'

At last a glimmer of hope:
    The Normandy landings,
    Hitler's armies pushed back,
    Paris relieved,
    Hitler's suicide.
The beginning of the end!

'You'll have to get a move on,' I said. 'Yes, I know, but I'm determined to get it finished for the Victory Parade.'

At last, a triumphant phone call – 'It's ready. I have just finished sewing it up. Come on over and have a look.'

_____

A few days later. . . .
    'Well, what do you think?'
    'Mmm, very nice!'
    'You seem a bit dubious – a bit on the big side?'
    'Well, I suppose it will allow for shrinkage.'
    'Mmm, that's a thought.'

_____

Weather forecast for the day of the Victory Parade: Very hot and sultry.

_____

The day after the Victory Parade. . . .
    'Hello Neville, how did the parade go?'
    'Fine, just fine.'
    'Did you wear Val's pullover?'

'Of course. My platoon and I caused quite a sensation.'

'Oh . . .' said I, all agog.

'In fact we got an extra cheer, me and my men, as we marched down Park Street. Me and my men, and all under one jumper!'

FOURTEEN

The End Of A Momentous Decade

The end of the 1930s seemed to tangle with the beginning of the '40s and so it was that this momentous decade came to a close. It was several years into the '50s before rationing and other restrictions were lifted.

My father, although in his late seventies, insisted on driving the van, almost within a week or so of his death, but with young Mavis acting as driver's mate. He was a man who but for the plummeting of the family fortunes only a couple of generations ago, would have been more suited to an academic life, a wise man, a great reader, a philosopher more at home in a garden than behind a counter, a 'Mary' to my mother's 'Martha', a gentle man, who taught me to see 'a world in a grain of sand' and a 'heaven' in a wild flower.

The 'forties has now passed into history and become part of the school curriculum, but when some of my young friends say, 'We rather envy you to have lived during those tremendous years,' I look back, and in spite of the hardships, the long hours and the shortages, I am rather inclined to agree.

PART THREE

WESTBURY VILLAGE
IN THE FIFTIES

Part Three
Westbury In The Fifties

Westbury Village In The Fifties   89
A Caring Society   91
The End Is In Sight   93
Free Gifts   94
The Garden That Bloomed At Christmas   95
The Golden Jubilee   101
Off With Her Head   102
Always On A Thursday   104
Snippets From Over The Counter   105
Farewell To Librae, Solidi, Demarii   107
Coffee With Love   108
Old Flo   109
Conversation With The Cleverdons   113
Our Village   116
Quiet Flows The Trym   117
Just An Afterthought   119

ONE

Westbury Village In The Fifties

Looking back with hindsight over the last forty years, it appears that the decade of the 'fifties acted as a bridge between the war-torn 'forties and the permissive 'sixties.

The 'forties with its terrors, threat of invasion, its shortages, the apprehensions, the exhilarations, and above all the camaradarie of its people, almost reluctantly drew to its close, for although the new decade beckoned, it was still a year or so before we could finally throw away our ration books. The people were war weary, and once the pressure was off, almost sank into lethargy.

You could, however, place an order for a new car, even if the wait was long, sometimes over a year, and driving tests, which had been abandoned during the war, were again introduced.

The 'unadopted' roads which were started before 1940 were now being completed. What memories of gingerly bumping along the Northovers, the East and Southovers, Hyland Grove and the Southdowns, first thinking of the tyres, so difficult to replace, then making sure the so precious egg ration in its flimsy paper bag was secure.

Shop-fronts of private houses could now be tarted up with a fresh lick of paint. What a joy to be able to buy a pair of nylons (a new word for the dictionary) without checking on your clothing coupons.

Oxo cubes went back to their original use, for kids no longer used their pennies to buy a cube to nibble, to eke out their sweet ration.

Some parents declared, 'We will see to it that our children will not suffer and be deprived as we were. We shall give them everything.'

Was that where things began to go wrong?

We no longer envied our compatriots who lived in a soft water area. 'Ought to have extra soap ration,' we argued. 'Our water is so hard.' Now we could have all the soap we needed, and sneak an extra bath without feeling guilty.

89

The trams had gone, to make way for the new means of transport, quicker but smellier. The village was surrounded by huddles of little cottages; these were condemned and the occupants shuffled off to the new Southmead Estate, with homes that had bathrooms and flush lavatories.

'It's very nice,' they said, then a wistful look came over their faces, 'but . . .!'

The old families in the gracious houses which ringed the village, and had been household names for many a year, either died out or moved into the country, as the new estates encroached more and more, and their homes eventually became schools and other institutions.

1953 saw the crowning of our Sovereign Lady, and a new 'Elizabethan' age was born. It heralded a new beginning and our hopes were high. Street parties were held, and home-made trimmings decked the streets and roads.

The wind of change was in the air – rumours, rumours. In 1954 our cinema, The Carlton, was razed to the ground, and in its place a new Phoenix was to rise, called a 'supermarket', launched by our own citizens, no less. Another import from the U.S.A. Why couldn't they stick to Spam?

The local shops, under the leadership of Bill Holliday of Mumfords' Stores, banded together to form a Trade Association for 'United we stand, divided we fall.' Thus we survived until retirement.

In 1957 Suez and petrol rationed again. More rumours, and the Patchway complex, with its bigger and bigger hypermarkets arose.

Thus the death knell tolled for the village shops, where once their owners carved out a living. Those shops over which children were born and some lived out their days, to be carried out, past the shelves of cornflakes, the Persil and Heinz baked beans, to their last resting place.

A voice over my shoulder as I waited at the checkout murmured, 'Why, oh why, did you ever leave?'

TWO

A Caring Society

How the ways of earning a living have changed as the twentieth century has progressed. The gentry had their butlers, their lady's maid, the cook, the parlour maid, housemaid, the tweeny, the humble scullery maid, plus the outdoor staff of coachmen, chauffeurs and gardeners; while the farmers, the shopkeepers and others had what was termed 'mother's help'. Amy was the first of Polly's, followed by Mabel, Ethel, Minnie, Doris, Lydia, Alice, Edith, Agnes and Dorothy. You can almost date an era by the Christian names, for not many have surfaced since then, but I must say I was surprised to see a pop star had named his baby 'Mabel', for, like mine, I had thought it had gone for ever.

The villagers had their families, the grans, the aunts, and kindly neighbours to call upon, some no doubt dubbed Nosy Parkers, and there was the gossip heard in the village shops. Customers were not just a 'faceless entity', passing through a check-out, but a person in their own right and treated as such.

I am now going to jump quite a few years to relate two incidents to show how a small community can become a caring one without the need of red tape.

MISS GAMMON

Margaret answered the phone, came over and said, 'It's Miss Gammon, she wants a quarter of tea sent up at once, is it all right if I just pop up? I won't be a minute.'

'O.K.' I replied; for the old lady, who lived in a cottage a few doors up the road, was very arthritic and housebound. A good half hour later a rush of footsteps announced Margaret's return.

'Where on earth have you been?' I queried, 'I was just about to send out for the town crier.'

'Well,' she rather breathlessly explained, 'she first asked me to skin a rabbit, then cut it up, and put it in the saucepan to cook; it was only for the blinking cat, and I hates the sight of blood.'

'Well, get cracking,' I said. The van is waiting to be loaded.

As she went to join the other girls, I heard her mutter,

'I bet she only asked for that tea just to get me up there.' I rather agree, don't you?

MISS JELLY

'Here,' said Dorothy, 'I haven't seen Miss Jelly for a day or so.' 'Neither have we,' chorused the others.

We were in the middle of a very severe patch of weather. The old lady was not one of the easiest to deal with, but she had had a very hard life. She lived in Shipley Road, in what was really a 'grace and favour' house, and her amenities were very sparse.

'I'll pop up and see if she is all right,' continued Dorothy, not stopping to put on a coat, although it was bitterly cold. She ran up the road, knocked on the door and the old lady appeared. 'Just wondered if you are all right, or can we get you anything?' asked Dorothy.

'Yes I am, and no you can't,' was the growled reply, and she promptly slammed the door in the face of one who was only trying to be a good samaritan.

Now, before you begin to tut-tut about such behaviour, there is a sequel. Some time later the old girl tottered into the shop, bearing a round-shaped parcel, wrapped in newspaper. She thrust it at Dorothy, muttered, 'This is for you; you can fetch the rest,' and then shuffled out. To the recipient's astonishment, and the merriment of her young colleagues, it proved to be a 'goes under', or to any of you who may say 'a what?' go and ask your grandmother, or better still, your great granny, for grandmothers seem to get younger every year. The old lady had realised that Dorothy was not being nosy, just trying to be helpful, so she looked around to see what she could spare from her meagre possessions and came down bearing her gift. But before you laugh, just ponder a moment. What does the good book say about 'the Widow's mite'?

Having read this, Dorothy mused, 'I wonder what happened to that set of bedroom ware? I reckon it would be worth quite a bit now.'

A friend, hearing this, said, 'It's unbelievable.' I assured her that it was true, for it would need a very vivid imagination to make it up. She agreed.

THREE

The End Is In Sight

There were smiles all round, for the end was in sight. No, no, not the end of the world. The end of rationing.

It had just been announced over the wireless that tea was coming off the ration, and tea was the very last item.

'Heard the news?' everyone was asked when they came into the shop, and if they hadn't, we soon told them.

'Let's hold a party,' said one, 'a bonfire in the garden.' (Black-out restrictions had long been lifted.)

'Yes, a party, and we can all throw our ration books in the flames, and jolly good riddance.'

'Won't Mrs Watts be pleased,' said Dorothy. Mrs Watts was one of our elderly customers. In fact she was well into her nineties when she died.

Tea rationing had been a terrible cross to bear for our Mrs Watts. Sometimes she would produce a half pound bag of sugar and ask rather diffidently,

'Do you think anyone would change this for a bit of tea?', and very likely we would find a sweet-tooth only too happy to oblige.

When the Food Ministry announced that citizens over a certain age would qualify for an extra 4 oz of tea a month, we thought she would be delighted. Not she. She wasn't going to let on how old she was, and it would be most indelicate for us to mention it.

However, the week that tea came off the ration, she still had one coupon left. I saw her with Mavis, their heads together, having a rather earnest conversation. My young assistant came over to me and said, 'Will you come over and explain to Mrs Watts that we don't need her coupon.'

The old lady was quite indignant. 'Mavis won't take my tea coupon and I've saved it special for this week.' 'But Mrs Watts, you can have as much as you like.'

'Yes, I know *that*, but I've got this coupon you see.'

As an aside I said, 'Take the coupon Mavis, and give her the tea.'

'Thank you, thank you,' beamed the old lady, as she walked out of the shop.

Well, after all, it was in the days when the customer was always right, and as for me, it was yet another good moment to savour.

FOUR
Free Gifts

'Was the dear old Mrs Watts, mentioned in your story about the "Henry Jones" flour our mother?' asked my friend Doreen, the fourth daughter of the family who once lived at Greenway Farm.

'Yes, it was,' I replied.

'How I remember,' she mused, 'sitting at the table, cutting out those "Henry Jones" signatures from the empty bags.'

It wasn't for the quality of the flour that our Mrs Watts insisted on having this particular brand, but the fact that by sending in sixty signatures you would receive a five shillings postal order.

Towel Soap became all the rage when ten wrappers entitled one to get a free towel. It took quite a bit of thought, deciding whether to choose a red, blue or green stripe.

Brooke Bonds brought out 'Divi' tea again – Five shillings (25p) for a completed card of stamps.

'Can I use this to pay my bill?' we were asked.

'What on earth are you doing?' I asked one of my girls, who had opened up a new case of cornflakes and was furiously taking out a packet at a time and scrutinizing each one. 'There's plenty on the shelf.'

'I know,' she said, 'but Mrs Flint wants a packet with an 'R' on to win a prize.'

'Oh! give me strength,' I thought.

94

'These free gifts are more nuisance than they're worth,' said Dorothy. 'I've just had such a ticking off from Mrs Blake because I didn't send a plastic basin with her blinking packet of Persil.'

What is it they say about THE RICH TAPESTRY OF LIFE?

During the time of rationing it was a case of bartering, – 'Anyone change this tea for a bit of sugar?' – but in the years to come it was the Battle of the Soap Barons.

Their first weapons were artificial flowers. It was a most embarrassing moment when a new customer from the Midlands thanked me for sending her a red rose with her first order. 'Never happened to me before,' she said.

I mumbled something, for she was so delighted, but how could I say it was free with her packet of Daz?!

FIVE

The Garden That Bloomed At Christmas

'Will you explain to Ivor our family relationship?' asked John Symons' daughter, Elizabeth, at my birthday party.

Now that posed a problem, for John, or rather Alfred, as we the family know him, had tried to work that one out many a time. There is a connection, and, however tenuous it is, I am glad, for over the years we have enjoyed many happy occasions together, too numerous to mention.

It was a typical murky November afternoon when the Symons' pulled up in Trym Road, opposite our shop, for it was in the days before yellow lines. Winnie, mother of Christopher and Elizabeth, tripped across the road, to complete her shopping and pay the

95

account. I accompanied her back to the car, and her husband quipped, 'Are you supposed to be early or late?'

I looked puzzled, and he pointed to the window box above the shop door, which one of the girls had filled with artificial daffodils. We had a laugh and they moved on.

Christmas Eve came, and I packed the boot of the car with all the left-overs from the various promotions. Dorothy and I attended the Midnight Communion service, and gave our thanks for the birth of the Christ child.

As we stepped outside the church, we beheld a white world, for snow had fallen. We set off for home, but stopped outside a certain house in Eastfield Road, and I nipped out and stuck an array of flowers all over the front garden, red roses, daffodils, delphiniums, sweetpeas, larkspur – the lot.

In the morning, Winnie looked out of the bedroom window and exclaimed, 'Whatever is the attraction? Everyone's stopping and looking in our garden.' (Everyone being the people on their way to the various churches.)

A phone call later, from 86 Eastfield Road, said 'Happy Christmas, and thanks very much.'

'I don't know what you mean,' I said, 'but Happy Christmas to you too.'

My brother Arthur, and I, standing where the petrol station in Falcondale Road now stands. The Rosery Tea Garden to the left behind us and Rosery Cottages to the right, c. 1924.

The Skyrme family visiting the Rowley family at East Hill Farm in their Austin 7 in 1927.

97

Canford Lane c. 1935. Carlton Cinema and cafe, which opened in 1933 and closed in 1959. The Spencer family owned the popular tea rooms at the bottom of the road.

The High Street c. 1956/7. W.H. Mogford and Sons store on the right – probably the best known shop in Westbury. The hut outside the Post Office was used for sorting the extra mail at Christmas time.

99

Celebrating 50 years as the village grocer. A party held at the British Legion Hall on October 13th 1959 for family, friends and customers.

SIX

The Golden Jubilee

'Miss Skyrme, what on earth do you think you are doing?'

I looked up on hearing that voice of authority, to behold a Chief Inspector of Police, resplendent in full dress uniform.

'What do you mean?' I queried.

'Your window display!'

Oh, that, it was quite a relief.

'It's our Golden Jubilee,' I told him proudly. 'My parents took over the shop on October 13th 1909.' It was now October 1959, and I had had the brainwave (or so I thought) to dress the window with everything bearing the name 'Golden' – Robertson's *Golden* Shred marmalade, *Golden* Syrup, *Gold* Label tea, Old *Gold* Chocolates, *Gold* Flake cigarettes, etc.

'I can see that!!' was his exasperated retort. 'But you are giving away lucky tickets, which may win a prize, and that amounts to a lottery, and it's illegal.'

'Oh! crikey!' I thought, and feared the worst.

'Now remove all those placards and posters at once and I'll forget I ever saw them. It's lucky for you I happened to be passing.'

Oh dear, and I had spent all the weekend writing them out.

What is it they say about 'the best laid plans of mice and men', but we didn't half sell some 'Golden Shred' marmalade.

SEVEN

Off With Her Head

'I'll have that one,' said the cook from The Hermitage, pointing to the large pork pie that took pride of place in the centre of our window display. 'Harris of Calne', the Wiltshire based firm famed for its choice West Country produce, especially their bacon, sausages and pies, were having a special week to promote their products. We had thought it quite a 'feather in our cap' when the lady at the big house gave us her custom for, after all, the £5 my parents paid for the stock when they took over the shop in 1909 included whips and tops, penny tin whistles and marbles at ten a penny, but we had progressed since those days.

'Nice day for the al fresco lunch,' remarked one.

'Yes, tis,' all agreed. It was quite a peaceful morning, everyone quietly getting on with their allotted jobs.

The peace was shattered by the shrill ring of the phone, someone sauntered over to answer it, gasped and beckoned to me. I took the receiver and nearly died on the spot. The cook's agitated voice told how, luckily, she had decided to cut the pie before sending it to table, and out poured a pile of sawdust.

I looked at a certain member of staff, and accusingly said, 'You didn't!!'

'Well,' spluttered the hapless one, 'she said she wanted that one.'

I uttered those words, now made famous by a certain M.P. 'Get on your bike.'

———————

Our friend was taking tea with us. I wish I could say we sat around a roaring log fire, but I'm afraid it was only a hissing gas one. 'Come up with any more memories?' she asked.

'Yes,' I said, and started to tell her the above story. Suddenly Dorothy, who usually sits back quietly listening, began to rock with laughter. Rosemary smiled indulgently and said, 'I know you worked so hard, and the hours were long, but you must have had fun.'

'Fun!' I said. 'That wasn't fun. It was near disaster.' At best I could

102

have been sent to the tower, at worst, I could have lost a valued customer.

Dorothy was still chuckling as I accompanied Rosemary to the door. On my return she was wiping the laughter tears from her eyes.

'Oh dear, oh dear. I'm sorry, but I keep picturing the cook's face when she cut that pie, but I'll tell you one thing,' she continued, 'the headache I've had all day is gone.'

It just proves one thing, 'Laughter is the best medicine.'

And furthermore, we didn't lose a customer.

EIGHT

Always On A Thursday

There was a regularity about life in the early part of the century for, as night always follows day, so it was that washing was done on a Monday. Friday night was 'Amami' night, or so the makers of the shampoo assured us.

It was also bath night for us youngsters, followed by a dose of Syrup of Figs (ugh) for 'clean without and clean within' was our parents' motto.

It was always on a Thursday that Mrs Weaver, the farmer's wife, who lived in the village of Over, drove into Westbury in her pony and trap. She pulled up outside the shop, and a chap loitering outside the White Lion would nip smartly across the road, only too willing to hold the horse's head for a couple of coppers, while she came into the shop to conduct her business.

She carried a tray, covered with a whiter than white cloth, containing her own farm made butter, each pat marked with the farm's emblem, and wrapped in a dock leaf, (a kind of early refrigeration). She would be asked into the room behind the shop, given a cup of tea and, her account paid, she would then buy her groceries in the shop, a very satisfactory arrangement all round.

Thus it was, that butter like Mrs Weaver's, and the eggs collected twice weekly from the local farms by my father, were just two of the attractions which brought what my country grandfather used to call 'the bettermus people' to the shop that once only sold marbles at 10 a penny.

NINE

Snippets From Over The Counter

'Oh, bother!' exclaimed the customer, as she peered in her handbag. 'I've left my purse behind. Can you lend me five pounds?'

'Certainly,' I said. I pressed the 'No sale' key and handed over the fiver.

'Oh good,' said she. 'Now I can pay your bill.'

I'm still trying to work that one out.

A young Norwegian lady brought her ration book in to register with us. She was staying with some of her compatriots, who had taken a house up at The Ridgeway.

Having written the details in the customer register, she was being given her rations. When it came to the preserves, I said in a very quick voice. 'Do you want jam on your jam ration or sugar on your jam ration, because you can have sugar on your jam ration or jam on your jam ration?'

Try saying that quickly, and you will understand why a bemused look came over the poor girl's face, and in a faint voice she said; 'I leave it to you, yes?'

'Serve the men first,' my mother always admonished. 'They've got work to go to.' Accordingly, whenever we spotted a man at the back, we promptly served him with his half ounce of baccy or whatever.

Thus it became second nature always to do likewise, until, crumbs, did I get a rocket from two irate women customers, who took umbrage. I thought I was going to be lynched. So yet another tradition hit the dust, for Women's Lib had come to our village.

Before the Second World War, it was rare to see a man doing the shopping. He usually only came to buy his baccy or fags, or maybe just a penny clay pipe.

Betty came away from the phone looking peeved.

'Just had a wigging from Mrs – because I sent her a blue toilet roll. Said it didn't go with her bathroom. Well, how was I to know? Wants a pink one sent up at once. She's got company coming.'

P.S. I wonder if her name was Mrs Hyacinth Bucket, pronounced Bou-kay.

P.P.S. Coloured toilet rolls had just hit the scene. Previously they were always white.

TEN

Farewell To Librae, Solidi, Demarii (or in other words, pounds, shillings and pence)

'Shall we ever be ready?' I asked myself, for when we had first heard the news that we were going to change into decimal coinage, it had seemed such a long way into the future, but now it was rushing towards us at a rate of knots. We were already marking our stock with two sets of prices: for example, 2/6 and 12½p, 1/- and 5p, and 6d and 2½p. The banks had issued the shopkeepers with a certain amount of 'New Money', so that we could familiarise ourselves with it.

An appointment had been made for an engineer to call and adjust the workings of the cash register. We watched with more than a hint of regret as our adding machine was carried out through the door of the shop – our little adding machine that had given us such sterling service (get it! sterling service), for it was going off to have its operation, an operation to have its £, s, d removed, in other words, its pounds, shillings and pence. When it came back it would only register pounds and pence. How dull, and how romantic the old names would soon begin to sound. A guinea = £1.1.0; a sovereign = £1.0.0; half a crown = 2/6; a shilling (a bob) = 1/-; sixpence (a tanner) = 6d; and the wee threepence piece (a thumber) = 3d.

During the weeks prior to 'D Day', we were bombarded with all sorts of gadgets and data supposed to help the changeover run smoothly, but for some it was all too much, and we overheard one of our elderly customers say to another, 'Why ever couldn't they have left it until all of us old uns had gone on?' We smiled sympathetically, but hadn't the heart to point out that whenever changes are made, there will always be some of us 'old uns'. That reminds me, is a metre more or less than a yard? See what I mean?

ELEVEN

Coffee With Love

'Come and have coffee,' said the voice over the phone. 'Remember Betty, who used to live a few doors up the road above your shop? Well, she's over from Canada and would like to meet you again.'

So I duly presented myself, to be greeted by my host, George Love, who later wagged his finger at me, saying,

'You never mentioned the Harriers in your book, did you?'

While I was 'er, er-ing', memories flooded back of Boxing Day mornings when the Harriers assembled outside the White Lion for the annual race, watched by myriads of locals.

While Betty smilingly dispensed coffee and cakes, George and I reminisced.

'Ah, yes, your brother Ted, yes,' he agreed, 'and Bill, my other brother,' then Bill Smith's face surfaced and Albert Clark and all the rest.

It should have been 'H' for Harriers, and Westbury in particular. Since those early days the club has progressed to even greater triumphs, and has become a name to be reckoned with in the athletic world, but nothing will take away the thrill of those Boxing Day runs. When young 'the sun shone all summer through', and Christmas weather was always 'bright, crisp and even' furthermore.

The runners were not only lads with numbers on their backs, we knew the Alberts, the Bills, the Charlies, the Erns, the Georges, the Joes, the Teds and the Walts, for they all lived in the village or just over the hill in Brentry.

But it wasn't half maddening when someone in the crowd gave you a nudge, thrust fourpence in your hand and asked, 'I don't suppose you could get me a packet of fags,' and you obligingly went and opened up the shop and missed the 'Off'.

Oh, well, as my mum would say, 'Just remember they are customers.'

TWELVE

Old Flo

'Old Flo wants a word,' said young Mabel.

'Oh bother,' said my mother, who was in the kitchen busy rolling out pastry. She wiped the flour from her hands and walked out into the shop. I followed, and stood beside her. By standing on tip toe I could just see old Flo, who was looking most uncomfortable. She shifted her weight from foot to foot, then blurted out, 'Can't pay my bill.'

'What is it this time?' said my mum in a resigned sort of voice, for this was the third week in succession that this had happened.

'Got to pay for the old man's boots to be mended,' she said.

'So you want me to pay for your husband's boots to be repaired,' said the shopkeeper.

'No, no,' said the indignant Flo. 'I'll pay but I can't pay you.'

'So how am I to pay my bills?' said the sorely tried Polly.

Old Flo sniffed, and began to list her trials and tribulations. The old man had spent the rent money down at the pub. The school board man had called because the kids had been playing hookey. The local farmer had caught one nicking apples from his orchard. Then she threw back her head and chortled, her open mouth showing two rows of rotting teeth, because she couldn't afford dental treatment. Then, with a grin, she exclaimed, 'It's enough to make a cat laugh i'nt it?'

'Well, we had better see what we can come up with,' said my mum. The solution was that she would pay the current week, then sixpence (2½p) each week off the arrears until the account was cleared. (It never worked.)

With a sigh my mother returned to the kitchen, and with a deeper sigh I again followed, for I had set my heart on a three-wheeled scooter. It was priced five shillings (25p) and I had calculated on my fingers that it would take ten weeks before I had any hope of getting it. Worst of all, my friend Mary, the Baker's daughter, already had hers.

Across the road at Sims, the bakers, the wife was surveying the long list of unpaid bills. 'It's no good,' she said. 'We shall have to put a stop on these accounts.' 'How can we?' replied her husband, Frank, who was a kindly man. 'Think of the little children.'

'Of course, you're right,' said his more practical wife, for she, like my mother, in spite of their seemingly tough exteriors, had very kind hearts. Together with Mrs Elling, the butcher's wife, these ladies made and sent good beef tea, nourishing soups and milk puddings to any of the ailing poor or any experiencing hard times.

Yes! They were kindly folk down our end of the village. I expect it was the same up at the top, but in those days it seemed a world away.

On the other hand, there may have been more needy folk down our end. Nevertheless, the families they reared were a fine example of upstanding, hardworking young people, and a credit not only to the village, but to the great world beyond.

Expo 1967 and my cousin Dorothy and I were in a coach, travelling to Montreal. We were staying with John Selby and his family in Toronto. John, the eldest son of our friends and fellow shopkeepers across the road, had emigrated to Canada in the early 'twenties.

It was the time of the 'Flower Children', and our courier sat on the floor, playing his guitar and singing the song, with its rather haunting, almost melancholy melody, 'Where have all the young ones gone?'

Today we could change the words to 'Where have all the small shops gone?' Well, I will tell you, they have been swept away, caught up in the backlash of the supermarkets and even bigger hypermarkets, with their garish fascia boards, windows plastered with special offers and cut prices, but above all, covering with concrete those little green oases where we played, ran races, made hay and held our village fêtes.

With the last of the little shops went the service, the friendly face, the doorstep delivery and the chance, when times were hard, for folk like Old Flo to put something on the slate.

Even I had forgotten, but I thank Mrs Elsie Bow, who, after all these years, has kept the Christmas card we sent to all our customers at Christmas 1959, and kindly sent me her copy.

The shop on the corner, so the big boys shout
Has had its day and is on its way out
But our 50th Christmas Skyrmes celebrate
And we're still hale and hearty we're glad to relate
So thanks, and God bless, as you pass on your way
And we trust we can serve you for many a day.
'Merry Christmas' from A.F. Skyrme and Staff.

How wrong can you be?

WESTBURY-ON-TRYM   9168

View from a field at East Hill Farm, with Westbury Church on the left. In the centre is the large white Georgian house of the college, by the trunk of the Scots Pine. This large house was burnt down in 1967 and Westminster Court Flats are now on the site.

THIRTEEN
Conversation With The Cleverdons

'A copy of your book, *The A.B.C. of Westbury Village*, was sent to the Fishers in America,' said my hostess, as she filled the coffee cups. She was remembering her old home, Trym Wood, the lovely house that nestles between fields and woods at the end of Trym Road.

'Did you know them?' she continued, but as they emigrated to the U.S.A. around about 1911, it was a little before my remembering time.

'Hassells, the coal merchant, is the first family that I remember,' I replied.

'Ah, yes,' smiled the former chatelaine, for they, too, were coal merchants. A most heartwarming account followed of a family who moved into Trym Wood in 1880, and how a son emigrated to the U.S.A. in 1906 and persuaded the rest of the family to follow in 1911. Although they came to love the vigorous young country of their adoption, and its people, memories like the first green shoots of spring kept surfacing, and of the old home they had left behind.

Quite a few years on, an agitated Mrs Fisher wrote. Was it true that her old home was going to be demolished? She was devastated at the thought.

A letter from the Cleverdons assured her that all was well. The house was in good hands and would be a joy for ever.

Thus commenced much correspondence and the start of a long and valued friendship between the families of the old home, with those across the sea. In one letter, a son wrote, 'My heart pants for Westbury, for, of all the many places I have lived, it is my love, and I live there in my mind every Christmas.'

Many visits were arranged, and each brother slept in the room where they were born, a room over the dining room, a room set aside for 'borning and departing' – how homely this sounds.

In 1984 son Edgar, now aged 97, and his kid brother Edward, aged

113

93, spent a holiday of a lifetime, returning to their roots after 78 years. They were royally entertained in their old home by the Mellor family. Edgar, ever mindful of a promise made to his mother, remained close to his religious training. He rode a bike, delivering meals to the elderly, until he was 99 years of age. He continued in good health, but quietly passed away at the age of 105 years in January 1993.

At the age of 94 years, and only a little time before her death, Mrs Fisher in one of her letters asked, almost wistfully, was the green and white holly tree they planted in the garden still there? Once again, she was reassured it was, and still flourishing on the banks of the river Trym, after over one hundred years, and very likely branches of it are used to decorate the old house at that very special time of Christmas.

———————

It was just a chance remark, 'Did you know the Fishers?' but what a happy outcome, and I thank those two chatelaines, Mesdames Cleverdon and Mellor, for allowing me to share some of their memories of a most remarkable old Westbury village family.

No! I didn't know the Fishers, but I wish I had.

What more fitting than that I should end my story of the place where I was born, lived, worked and played, in that very spot where those little cottages that nestled under the shadow of our ancient church and its one time adjoining monastery, were built and must have formed the nucleus of the village we now think of as our very own.

It was from there we drew our first customers, from there that the fresh young lad from Somerset, who became my dad, first met those young men who became his pals, and with whom he played pranks on the unsuspecting village folk, pranks that now seem so innocuous compared with those of today. In manhood, these same young men worked side by side, tending their allotments on Henbury Hill, thus providing fresh vegetables for their families.

I slip back in time, and in my mind, I am accompanying my aunt and her two young daughters up Trym Road, for it is August, and it is imperative to place an order for the winter's fuel. To order your coal in August was as traditional as 'the 12th' is to grouse shooting, and in any case, the early birds received preference. As an added incentive, a special discount was given.

The four of us crossed the road from the shop and started upon our journey. The first cottage we passed, with its old world garden, was once the home where Peg Sawyer and her siblings were born and

114

raised. Beyond the vegetable garden the steep field, (now Walton Rise) rose to its giddy height, but just over the stone wall at the bottom, the clucking of hens and the grunts of contented pigs could be heard; often the air would echo with the laughter of children, for not only were the Sawyer children blessed with loving and caring parents, they had space to run, to play, to help with the animals, have picnics, build bonfires, and slide down the steep field when snow lay on the ground.

The next landmark was 'The Malt House', once so ably kept by the Pearse family. The remembrance of their home cooked ham on the bone and famous farm cheeses must even now cause many a mouth to water. We were impressed with the Dial House, glanced up Channel's Hill, where once the carriages and wagons trundled on their way to the Passages, to catch the Packet boat and cross over to Wales.

It is pleasing to the eye that the little cottages, with their pretty gardens, still cluster around, even more so that at least two are still occupied by sons and daughters bearing the names of those truly good old village families remembered from my earlier days, the Derretts and the Wembridges.

To view all this on a sunny summer evening from the vantage point outside the old 'Vic' Inn, especially when the Trym is in its sparkling mood, must be most relaxing. With a little imagination, this village scene could rank equal with any of the beauty spots in the lovely and picturesque county of Cornwall.

After much deviation, we arrived at Hassel's the Coal Merchant, the object of our walk. I wonder if my remembrance is a true one, or is it coloured by the passing of over seventy years, but as my aunt unlatched the heavy iron gate, it was more like entering a farmyard than that of a coalyard. All around were outhouses and stables, the sounds of clucking hens, and, in the distance the quacking of ducks. Carts and wagons littered the yard, but yes, it was the right place, for over against the walls were piles of the stuff my father called 'black diamonds'.

In response to my aunt's knock on the door, someone appeared, and after a friendly greeting and a chat, it was down to business. The two orders were given, and whatever went before, it always ended, 'and 5 cwt of Coalpit Heath, small, please.'

FOURTEEN
Our Village

It was a Sunday morning, and I was hurrying up the road, for Val would be waiting on the corner of Church Road. We were going to church. Suddenly a car pulled up, the driver opened the window and called out, 'Excuse me, but can you tell me where the White Horse is?' 'Right here,' I said, pointing to the pub of the corner.

I later told my brother about this incident. He roared with laughter and said, 'Not that White Horse you daft kid.'

I was a bit miffed, as I didn't like being laughed at, but it explained the look on the driver's face.

Westbury as a name is hardly pretentious. It doesn't have the same kind of ring to it as say Bourton-on-the-Water, Selworthy Green, or The Mull of Kintyre, and there are many Westbury's up and down the country, but ours is distinguished by the 'on Trym'.

FIFTEEN

Quiet Flows The Trym

'I think I shall call my book, "Quiet flows the Trym,"' I said. 'Rather apt don't you think?'

'Not always so quiet,' said Rosemary Mellor of Trymwood, remembering when the river rose so high it flowed through the house and ruined her dining room curtains.

'Not always so quiet,' said Barbara Doré from her home perched high above the Trym. 'This very morning I can hear it roaring from right up here.'

No, not always so quiet thought I, suddenly remembering the times of great storm, and we down at the shop became Westbury-*in*-Trym.

Life is a bit like a river. It has a beginning and an ending. Sometimes it is so placid it almost becomes boring, sometimes it sparkles as the sunlight hits the crystal clear water and the river ripples over the stones lying on its bed in joyous abandonment. At other times it breaks out, by bursting its banks, and like a marauding army, spreads devastation and despair, then, just as abruptly, rejoins the straight and narrow, and the water, however muddied, clears, and is soon its sparkling self again.

I found it most rewarding that my previous writings evoked such happy, if sometimes almost wistful memories in the boys and girls who had left the village scene for lands far across the sea.

I thought I would try my hand at summing up their thoughts in a line or two, discovered I was no Rupert Brooke, but, for what they are worth, here they are:

Do Kids Still Paddle In The Trym?

'Home, now is here', for we've travelled far,
Two sons, a girl, and the latest car,
But often I have a recurring dream
Of standing by a village stream
So I write to ask, tis but a whim,
Do kids still paddle in the Trym?

Pauline Bicknell and
Rene Mogford with Peg
Selby, who was on a
visit from Canada,
standing on the bridge
over the Trym, where
Hilsdon Road and
Merlin Close is now.

SIXTEEN

Just An Afterthought

How many rueful smiles have been smiled, how many sighs of exasperation or resignation, by almost every owner of a small shop when yet another whispered aside has been heard, 'It must be a little gold mine.'

But I'm afraid I have to tell you that being so haphazard, and with the tendency to give a party at the drop of a hat, I never did find that gold mine. It was a case of, 'Help, help, has anyone seen my pick and shovel?'

But I did have fun.